Beginner
+
Intermediate Guide
to Whittling

Ryan Feldman

the information contained within this document, including, but not limited to, errors, omissions, or inaccuracies.

Table of Contents

Beginner's Guide to Whittling

What Beginner Wood Carvers Need to Know to Start Whittling

Ryan Feldman

Introduction

I took a step back and admired my handiwork. The shark was slightly larger than the other fish, but it fit perfectly into the open space on the shelf. After traversing the forest the previous weekend, I had found a beautiful piece of basswood just begging to be whittled into something new. I sat under the shade of the big oak tree while whittling away until finally, the shark emerged from the depths of the wood. It was magnificent! I had finished my aquarium scene but already knew my next whittling project would be an owl. Even though I had only been whittling for a few months, I could not wait to get back to the forest soon and find another piece of wood.

"Being creative is not a hobby, it's a way of life."
- Unknown

I grew up in the Pacific Northwestern forests. I had free reign and often spent time wandering through the forest. Sometimes I got lost... That is okay because eventually, I would find my way back home. One thing was consistent though - I always came home with pieces of wood. The textures, shapes, and possibilities intrigued me. Wood was beautiful, and knowing that it can transform into so many things made me wonder what I could do with it. From a very young age, I knew that working with wood was in my genes. Today, I consider myself to be a bit of a "lumberjack" because I became a carpenter who builds homes. Yet, my wood carving hobby is fruitful too - it has become a lucrative side hustle.

Whittling is a creative pastime, which quickly becomes part of a person's lifestyle. For me, whittling was a saving grace. As a teenager, I found myself engaging in illegal behavior. I was using drugs and committing crimes. My life was spiraling out of control, and I could easily have gotten myself into even stickier situations. I knew this unruly version of myself was not the person I wanted to be as an adult. Luckily, my love for nature drew me back to reality. I spent more time carving wood, which made me understand just how powerful this form of art is for my life. Working with wood and being in the forest gave me a sense of purpose: I finally felt at home and knew I could contribute to society through my natural affinity for woodwork.

Sometimes, a person wants to try something new, but you just don't know where to start. There are a myriad of ideas on how to spend your time, what hobbies to try, and why one hobby is better than the next. I have always been creative - it already manifested in me as a young child roaming the woods and dreaming about all kinds of creatures and treehouses. Yet, as a man, I wanted a creative hobby that still reflected my masculinity; although, it is perfectly suited for a woman's hobby too. Whittling made sense to me. It is a quintessential outdoor activity that conjures images of a flannel-clad individual using a pocket knife to shave wood slivers off a stick.

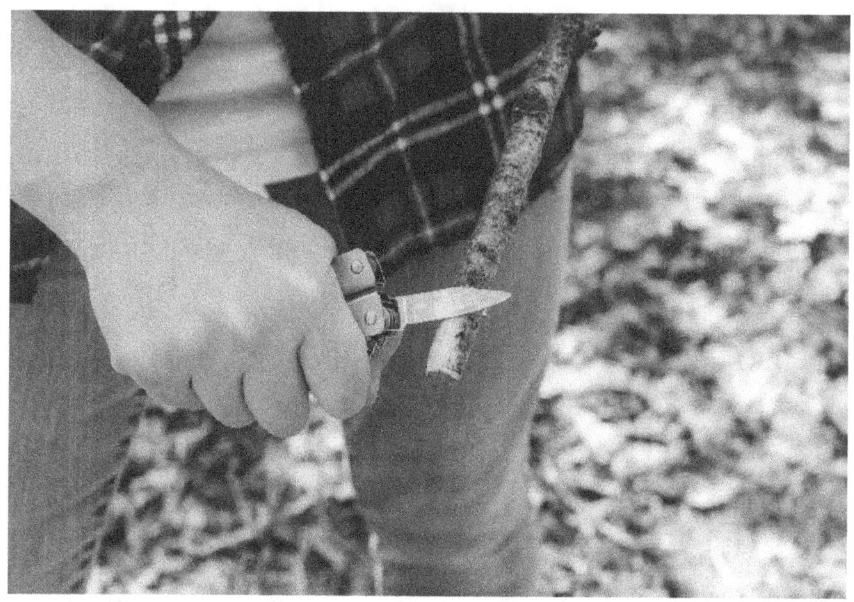

I want to share my passion for whittling with you! I didn't know everything about wood carving from the start. At first, I only had a basic knowledge of whittling, but as I practiced more, I gained confidence in my hobby. Mistakes were part of the process, and I often started over because the project was not going according to plan. Yes, it was frustrating, but it was a valuable learning experience. I was getting to know my craft. I found out the best type of wood to use for whittling and the most suitable tools. Sometimes, I thought I knew what I wanted to make, but soon the wood indicated a different direction. Some of my most prized pieces came from projects that took on a life of their own. Now, I am a master whittler and you can be too!

So, why should you start whittling? Maybe you have a lot of time on your hands, you recently retired, or you are recovering from an operation. It might be the holidays and you want to learn a new skill. Even if you are only going camping for a weekend, whittling is a great activity.

Whittling enables creative expression and is a productive way to spend your time. It prevents you from taking part in "harmful" hobbies as I did since whittling keeps you busy. Whittling is a fun activity that you can share with your family and friends. It is the perfect activity that you can learn while teaching it to your children.

One of the things I like most about whittling is that it is an activity without a specific location or a bunch of equipment. You can whittle at home or sit around the campfire while whittling. I enjoy going for a hike to find a piece of wood and then whittling next to the lake. You can even whittle indoors using a dedicated workspace or in front of the fireplace (although this area might need extra cleaning afterwards). If the bug bites, you might just start a small income-generating business from your hobby. I want to empower you with the knowledge to start whittling since it has so many benefits.

Whittling is easy to learn. Some people find whittling confusing and believe you need specialized tools. It is not as difficult as you might think. All you need are the right tools, patience, and some time to master the techniques. In this book, I teach you the basics, but steadily progress into advanced concepts. I also discuss all the knives and other tools suitable for whittling, so you will have clarity before starting projects. Each technique is detailed in plain language to make understanding easier. You will be able to apply these techniques effortlessly. If you ever get stuck, simply go back to the relevant chapter and revise the concepts. Remember, practice makes perfect.

Whittling skills are suitable for all ages, from children to the elderly. You do not need any advanced training or knowledge. Using my techniques, your talent develops quickly, and complex carving projects are within your reach much faster! The last chapter is an added bonus: I will teach you how to make money from whittling projects.

What are you waiting for? Let's get started with the basics!

Chapter 1:
The Most Creative Fun Ever

I cannot imagine a better way to express myself than through whittling! It is the absolute best way to channel creative energy. Whittling allows you to use your spare time productively and creatively, which stimulates your brain. While improving your mental and physical health, creativity also gives you self-confidence and socialization skills. There are so many benefits that make creative expression essential for a good life.

Being creative can make you happier! Artistic activities usually require repetitive motions that work together towards an end result. As you work, you get into a rhythm, which is called flow. This flow helps maintain focus, and you might not even realize the passing time because you are absorbed in your task. Flow creates relaxation, reduces your heart rate, and decreases anxiety levels. Seeing results from creative tasks releases dopamine, a hormone that makes you feel good, which becomes a motivating force for future activities.

Creativity boosts your mental health and has a positive impact on your self-esteem. A healthy mind is essential to living your best life, so you should engage in activities that improve your mental health. Creativity calms your brain because you focus on a specific task and often forget about everything else. Doing something artistic is similar to meditation as repetitive motions align with your breathing patterns. These effects help with the release of dopamine, which reduces stress and depression. Creative activities, like whittling, can help in processing trauma or emotions as it allows you to express yourself without using words.

Many creative activities encourage social interaction, which is necessary for a balanced life. Some art forms, like painting, are done on your own, while others, such as music ensembles, require groups. Regardless, any type of creative activity can be shared with family and friends by teaching them a new hobby or simply showing them your work. Whittling is great for socialization because you can teach others or just spend time in their company while working on a piece. Social skills also make you a better communicator, improve your mood, and enhance your mental health.

Expressive activities have an impact on your cognitive abilities. Any form of creativity - painting, writing, playing music, whittling, and so on - can make you smarter. Your right brain focuses on the flow, while your left brain powers your movements. When you partake in creative activities, both sides of your brain are working and communicating with each other. This communication strengthens your brain and ability to understand complex things.

Speaking of the mind, did you know that creativity alleviates dementia? Individuals with dementia often forget things or become frustrated easily, but art helps in lessening their symptoms. Time spent creatively generates feelings of belonging and reduces social isolation resulting from dementia. It alleviates stress and frequently helps a person to remember their true personality traits. Creativity uses all your senses, so it stimulates the senses of dementia sufferers, which help them to remain sharp.

Whittling is the perfect hobby for you! Creative hobbies are great for people with an artistic flair. Even people who consider themselves to lack creativity can do whittling. There are so many benefits to creativity that it only makes sense to do something creative. Now is the time to start being creative if you are not already, and if you are the artistic type, then try whittling as a new expressive form!

What is Whittling?

Whittling is a type of art where a person uses a knife to shave wood slivers from a larger piece of wood. Usually, the knife has a small, straight blade and many people only ever use a folding pocket knife for their whittling. Some people simply whittle away at the wood by shaving off pieces aimlessly. However, a better form of whittling uses these shaving techniques to create artworks or usable wooden objects.

There are subtle differences between whittling and woodcarving. Whittling is seen as using a knife to carve a piece of wood. So, in a sense, you could consider whittling as a technique used in woodcarving. However, woodcarving uses various tools, in addition to knives, to create an object from wood. These tools may include power tools, chisels, and mallets. Another small difference is that whittling requires you to hold a piece of wood in your hand, while woodcarving includes larger projects where handheld wood becomes unsuitable. Think about it this way, a whittler can create a small eagle, while a person that carves wood can produce an entire, life-size totem pole. It does not matter which type of woodcraft you prefer, just ensure that you enjoy it!

Whittling is one of the cheapest and most accessible hobbies you will ever come across. All you need to get started is a piece of wood and a knife. You probably already have both those items available to you or you can obtain them easily. Most people own some sort of hobby knife or a pocket knife. Finding wood is not an issue either - walk around your neighborhood or visit your local park to find some wood. Always check whether you can pick up or cut pieces of wood in a specific area. If there is no other alternative, then visit a local hardware store for wood. Whittling really is an inexpensive hobby, so have a look in and around your home for supplies.

Five Reasons Everyone Enjoys Whittling

Here are another five reasons why whittling is enjoyable, just in case you are still not convinced it is for you.

1. It is a pleasurable pastime. Whittling allows you to forget about all your worries and just focus on your project. It relaxes you but becomes addictive because you want to continue once the object starts to take shape in front of you. Many people spend hours whittling. As the saying goes: time flies when you are having fun.

2. You can make your own house decor. Whittling decorations is a great use of your skills because you can add a project to a bookshelf, kitchen counter, or office. These decorations are personal and might even motivate you because you know you can do anything you set your mind to. Just imagine the Christmas ornaments you could whittle for the tree.

3. Family and friends will receive personalized gifts. People appreciate a handmade gift more than a store-bought item. Whittling is a chance to create a personalized gift for someone you know. Most likely, you have a good idea of what the person likes (for

example, trees or cats) so use that as inspiration for the present you will whittle.

4. Cleaning up is easy and environmentally friendly. Whittling creates wood shavings or chips but not the fine dust associated with other activities. Your clean up time is very short because you just need to sweep the shavings together and discard them. Add the shavings to the trash, a compost heap, or use them as fire starters.

5. Your fine motors skills improve over time. Holding wood and a knife requires attention and motor skills, which are the small movements made by using your hands. Whittling can improve these skills and increase your hand-eye coordination.

History of Woodcarving

Woodcarving has been around since the dawn of time. During prehistoric times, wood carvings played a part in rituals. Christians used wood to carve religious figures and symbols, such as crosses. Unfortunately, many wooden art pieces succumbed to the elements as wood is perishable. About 11,000 years ago, the *Shigir Idol* was carved and is one of the oldest wooden sculptures still in existence. Artists in the Middle Ages also conveyed religious stories through woodcarving, since the church dictated what imagery was allowed in public. Many ancient churches feature elaborate wood carvings of the Last Supper or saints in their interior decor. The *Holy Bloody Altar* by Tilman Riemenschneider and the *Gero Crucifix* are two of the most prolific religious wood carvings. The Louvre in France holds the *Mary Magdalene* created by Gregory Erhart during 1500.

The Renaissance brought about several wood-using artists, although it was not a popular medium. Following the idea of one universal man by Leon Battista Alberti, many artists produced busts or portraits to capture a lifetime image. Artists such as Donatello continued to work with wood and created masterpieces like *St John the Baptist* and *Penitent Magdalene*. Yet, wood was not always a good choice because people knew it would decompose over time.

Classical times saw marble becoming a frontrunner for sculpture. However, many decorative designs came from wood, which was used frequently for ornaments. In England, a school of woodcarving by Grinling Gibbons became a famous institution. During the 18th century, wood was a popular medium for carving cherubs, door panels, and mantelpieces. Some European schools also included woodcarving as part of the curriculum.

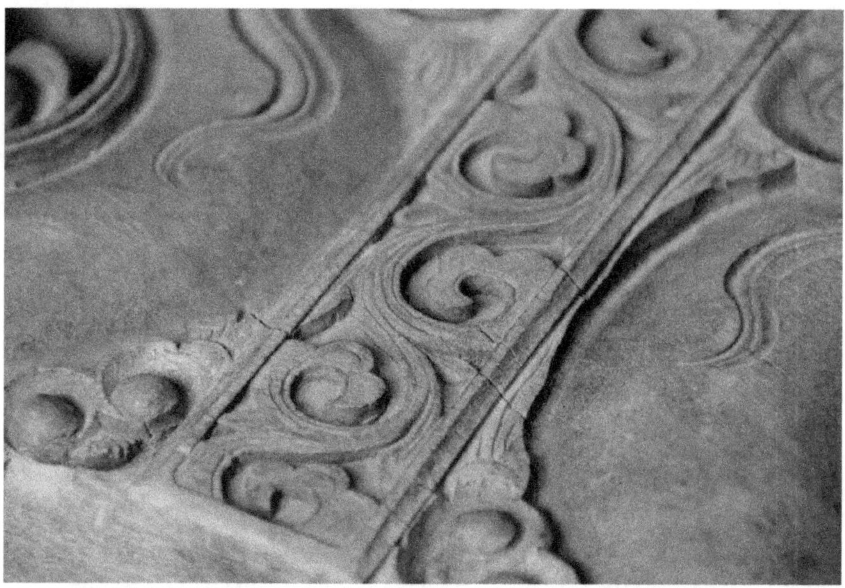

Woodcarving remained popular throughout modern and contemporary times. Wood featured in many sculptures, masks, votives, and ornamental furniture. Some of the most prolific artists during these times include Louise Nevelson, Paul Gauguin, and Henry Moore. Modern art museums often display wooden pieces such as the *Porcupine Cabinet* by Sebastián Errázuriz and the *Nest Chair* by Nina Bruun. Wood has been a popular medium throughout the centuries and remains useful today. It is used across all continents and the natural grain makes for textural artworks that delight the senses.

What to Know Before You Start

Whittling is fun and easy, but you need to know a few basic things before starting any project. A knife is your first resource. Although pocket knives work well, you might want to purchase a speciality whittling knife. There are various types of knives discussed in Chapter 2. Keeping your knives sharp is important too, so a strop or sharpening stone forms part of your basic supplies. Secondly, you will need wood to whittle. Basswood is a popular choice because it has less grain and the softer texture makes it easy to carve. Other frequent choices include balsa wood or pine. An in-depth look at wood is given in Chapter 4. You can even use some twigs or small branches for whittling, which is a great option if you just want to practice the basic whittling methods.

Always start your whittling projects with the end product in mind. Think about the size of your finished product and the supplies you require. Make sure you get a piece of wood that is large enough for your whittling project and ensure your knife remains sharp throughout the process.

Protective Gear

Any activity has its risks and whittling is no different. With knives, there is always a danger of cutting yourself. Wood can splinter and lodge into the skin or shavings can hurt you. There are precautions you can take to prevent injuries.

Gloves are essential for whittling and preventing injuries. Gloves should meet EN 388 (European) standards for safety. They should be resistant to abrasion, not be cut through easily, tear, or puncture. Of course, repetitive use will wear gloves out eventually. Always look for gloves with the EN 388 mark and you can feel safe knowing that your gloves are tested for durability.

Thumb guards and protective eyewear can help too. A thumb guard goes over the thumb to help keep it injury-free, especially since a lot of pressure comes from this digit while whittling. It has a similar purpose to gloves but adds extra security to avoid getting splinters, blisters, or cuts. Safety glasses also help as any wood shavings or chips that jump towards you will bounce off the eyewear rather than lodging in your eye.

Using safety equipment is a personal choice. Not all whittlers use these items but it is up to you to decide your level of protection. A cut from a knife can sever your fingers, especially if a lot of force was applied to the blade. A piece of wood in your eye can also injure it for life. Rather to be safe than lose a finger or your eyesight to a silly injury. Remember, you cannot whittle if you have an injury so always look after yourself, regardless of whether you use protective gear or not. Always make an informed decision and ensure your protective equipment meets local or international safety standards.

Disclaimer

Whittling is a hands-on activity and cuts are inevitable. The author and publisher can not be held liable for any injuries incurred during whittling or using this book. The use of protective gear is recommended to safeguard against injuries but you could still hurt yourself. Always take the necessary precautions when doing whittling-related activities. Children engaging in whittling should be supervised by an adult at all times.

What Makes Whittling Different?

Whittling is a hobby and craft, yet it also differs from other pastimes. It benefits the body by reducing your blood pressure, heart rate, and stress. The rhythmic motions bring calm and your breathing soon matches the cutting strokes. This repetition is not always possible in other hobbies and some sports increase your heart rate and blood pressure. Whittling also lets you practice mindfulness. When you remain in the moment and experience an activity with all your senses, then you are being mindful. So focusing on whittling alone and forgetting about everything else is a mindful activity. Whittling connects you with nature and makes you pay attention to it by walking to find wood. It reminds us of the spiritual connection we have with the world since trees are also living organisms. Whittling makes you realize why it is important to look after natural resources.

Woodcarving is a traditional hobby that you can pass along many generations. Once a person knows how to whittle, this craft is taught to children, grandchildren, and other family members. Many families cherish items carved out of wood and these artworks become family heirlooms, which creates a connection transcending time and space.

Whittling builds trust and self-esteem. Although measurements and technique form part of woodcarving, there is a lot more emphasis on getting a feel for the word and letting your mind guide the process. This emphasis enables you to trust your gut instinct more and builds your self-esteem as you grow in your whittling journey. As you improve your whittling skills, you also become more confident in other activities and sometimes your stress disappears entirely because you believe you can do it. Whittling is one hobby that always builds up a person, is good for your health and wellbeing, and has a positive impact on your traditional work.

Whittling provides so many life-changing opportunities! There is great breadth and potential in whittling, which should make you want to pick up your supplies and get going. Now is the time to harness all your creative energy and transform it into productive action! If you think you understand the basics in this chapter, then let's get a better look at the tools of the trade. It is almost time to get carving!

Chapter 2:
Know Your Tools

Just like any other hobby, you want to ensure that you understand what it entails. You need to know what tools you require, the basic concepts, and relevant materials. Whittling includes a series of tools, which can be used as an extension of your mind. These tools help in bringing your artwork to life. For this reason, it is important to understand the tools and their functions properly before you start whittling. Taking care of your tools is just as important, so let's have a look at all this equipment.

There are three basic tools that every whittler needs in their arsenal. Firstly, you need knives. A knife is a tool you will use to carve your artwork by shaving away pieces of wood. The second tool is gloves to protect your hands from being cut or becoming sore while whittling. Finally, your hands are an essential tool in whittling. Your hands hold the wood, apply pressure to the knife, and help to get a feel for your project. Every whittler requires these three sets of tools. An overview of this equipment helps in understanding the best tools for the job.

Whittling Knives

Woodcarvers often have many knives and interesting tools at their disposal. However, a whittler usually only has a few select knives. Some whittlers only own one knife, while others have several knives to use for different techniques.

Simple Pocket Knife

A simple pocket knife is the quintessential whittling tool. Most whittlers think of a pocket knife as their first piece of whittling equipment. A pocket knife consists of a sharp blade, sometimes more than one, that folds into the handle. The blades are made from strong steel. A surgical steel or carbon steel blade is best as these blades are durable and strong. Some pocket knives have stainless steel blades but these are not as strong, so might not be the best option. The handles are usually made from wood, although some may have a metal or acrylic inlay.

A pocket knife is important for basic whittling. It is a sharp knife that makes various strokes, including pushing, pulling, shaving, and chipping. It usually has a round sharpish point. A pocket knife is the basis for all whittling projects, so invest in a proper knife with an ergonomic handle that fits your hand comfortably. It is best to choose a pocket knife that has a locking mechanism to keep the blade securely open during use and tightly closed when put away.

A pocket knife works well for whittling because you can take it anywhere. Some pocket knives feature a belt clip so you can connect the knife to your belt for easy carrying. Folding the blade away makes it safe for you to carry the knife in your pocket. A pocket knife can be sharp and cut you easily. Always check that the blade is folded in properly and close the knife carefully.

A pocket knife is great as you can whittle as soon as you find a piece of wood or even a twig while camping, which is not the case for some of the other knives. Most people already own a pocket knife for camping and general purposes, so all you need to do is pick up some wood and start whittling!

Flat Steel Blade

A flat steel blade is another essential knife for whittling. These knives usually have a fixed blade housed in a wooden or metal handle. Approximately 3-4" in length, flat steel blades end in a sharp, thin point made from carbon steel or similar materials. Its rounded middle section makes this knife useful for many purposes. Some flat steel blade knives come with a protective sheath, usually made from leather, to store the blade safely when not in use.

A flat steel blade is a universal tool for whittling. The round middle works well to slice the wood and create deep cuts. A rolling motion is possible with the rounded blade. The sharp point of the blade allows you to make intricate designs or delicate cuts in small or tight areas.

Flat steel blades are slightly longer and very sharp. Choose a knife with a comfortable handle, otherwise, it may slip in your hands resulting in cuts. Ensure you have a protective cover for the blade to avoid injuries. A flat steel blade is fantastic for whittling and, with some practice, you will soon use this knife with confidence. Making ornamental cuts and fine details with a flat steel blade makes it stand out from other whittling knives.

Hook Blade

This whittling knife looks exactly like it sounds. The blade is shaped like a hook. Think about Captain Hook with his steel arm hook - that is exactly the shape of this knife. The blade may be sharpened on one or both sides of the hook. Some hooks come to a sharp point, while others have a flat, square edge. A hook knife can injure you, so be careful when using one, especially since both the round edges and endpoints can be very sharp.

A hook blade is necessary if you want to cut round shapes, which makes this knife unique. For example, you might whittle a spoon or bowl and a normal blade just cannot create the hollow into the wood. Now, you have to remember that there is a big difference between the hollow areas in a spoon and bowl. Some hollows are very shallow but wide, others are deep, and some hollows very small and round. For this reason, the diameter of the hook blade differs. Think about the projects you plan on attempting and what type of hook blade is best for your objectives. Purchase a single hook knife to start with and purchase others as you start on new projects.

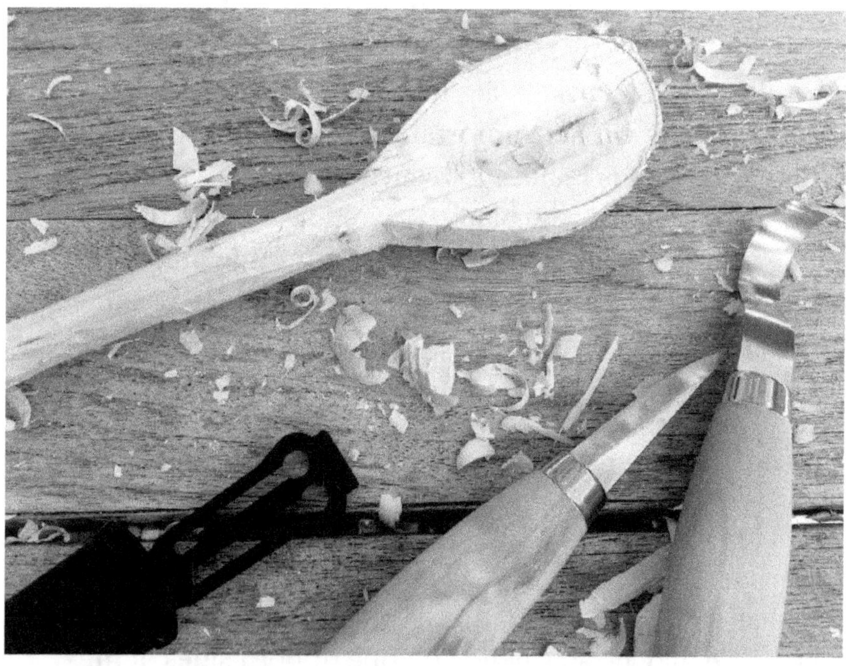

Raindrop Razor Edge

A raindrop razor edge is a very sharp and versatile knife. The blade looks like part of a raindrop - it has a rounded edge but the actual cutting section is quite straight. A raindrop razor edge has a very sharp pointing end. Some raindrop razors are folding knives and the blade folds into the handle. Others have a fixed blade in a wood, metal, or enamel handle.

A raindrop razor edge is a versatile knife. It is used for cutting strokes, shaving wood slivers, and making deep cuts. The sharp point lets you burrow into the wood to create fine details and small holes. The blades are sturdy making this knife adaptable for many purposes. A rainbow razor edge has the advantage of having a flat blade and sharp point, making it suitable for a variety of whittling projects.

The handles of some raindrop razors are quite small and make these knives difficult to use. A small handle can cause blisters or chaff marks. In some cases, the handle may slip and cause injuries. Take your time when searching for a raindrop razor edge, so that you find one that works for your hands. Some people wrap extra leather around the handle, making it slightly larger and easier to handle.

There are so many knives available for whittling. Start by looking at the Morakniv brand, which are high quality and durable knives. Choose knives that feel good in your hands. You want to pick a knife that is comfortable and usable for many hours without hurting your hands. There is nothing worse than using a knife that creates blisters or sore spots.

Are you ready to go buy a knife? Great! Do some research and select knives suitable for your projects.

Remember though, that knives can cut more than just wood - it might just cut you!

Protective Wear

Whittling injuries are a normal part of the learning process. Avoid cuts on your hands by protecting them. Gloves and finger guards are the best protection from cuts, grazes, and blisters. There are various types of gloves available, so think carefully about the best fit for you.

Cut-resistant Gloves

Cut-resistant gloves are an inexpensive and basic option for small whittling pieces. These are perfect for beginners and comfortable for longer wear. Gloves come with a cut resistance rating - opt for a higher rating as it means they are more resistant to blades. Kevlar is a popular material for these gloves.

Cut-resistant Gloves with No-slip Grip

A no-slip grip is an added feature on some cut-resistant gloves. Usually made from Kevlar, these gloves have rubber on the palms and fingers. Rubber dots on the palms and fingers make it easier to remain dexterous. Alternatively, the whole palm and insides of the fingers have a rubber coating but it makes the gloves stiff until you have used them several times. The rubber gives you a better grip when holding tools or pieces of wood.

Leather Palms

Some gloves have leather palms and leather over the inside of the fingers. These gloves are similar to the no-slip grip gloves, but they are comfier. Leather palm gloves are very stiff when they are new. Using them often softens the leather and makes these gloves some of the best ones to use for whittling.

Steel Wire Gloves

Steel wire gloves are similar to the normal cut-resistant gloves. The fabric used in making these gloves are interwoven with fine steel wire. This wire makes the glove slightly more rigid and improves its resistance to blades. Some of the steel wire gloves feature rubber palms or dots to improve the grip.

Metal Mesh Gloves

Metal mesh gloves are a great choice if you are worried about cutting yourself. These gloves are strong and because the entire glove is woven with thin metal. Metal mesh gloves are rigid and can make it a bit more challenging to hold onto the wood. Metal mesh gloves are available for normal workshop wear but some brands offer ones specifically for woodcarving.

Shop Gloves

Shop gloves are commonplace in most homes. Suitable for traditional DIY or workshop activities, these gloves come in many fabric choices and thicknesses. Most shop gloves are not cut-resistant, so your gardening gloves might not work so well for whittling. Still, shop gloves do give some protection if you cannot afford whittling gloves at the moment.

Finger Guards

A finger guard only protects certain fingers rather than your whole hand. Guards are available for all fingers, although thumb guards are most common for whittling. A finger guard is ideal if you want to grip your equipment properly or if you just want some protection to whittle while you are away from home. Some people attempt a cheap option by wrapping some athletic tape around their fingers but this strategy provides very little protection.

Glove Comparison

So many gloves, which ones to choose! Here is a handy comparison chart to help you make a decision about the best option for you.

	Pros	**Cons**
Cut-resistant gloves	<ul><li>Inexpensive</li><li>Comfortable</li><li>Usable on either hand</li><li>Cooler than other gloves</li></ul>	<ul><li>Can puncture</li><li>Wood shavings stick to gloves</li><li>Frays with use</li></ul>
Cut-resistant gloves with a no-slip grip	<ul><li>Affordable</li><li>Comfortable</li><li>Better grip on wood</li><li>Fewer wood shavings sticking to gloves</li></ul>	<ul><li>Can puncture</li><li>Hands become warm</li><li>Feel stiff</li><li>Rubber wears off</li><li>Frays with use</li></ul>
Leather palms	<ul><li>Comfortable</li><li>Durable</li><li>Slightly safer than normal gloves</li></ul>	<ul><li>Can puncture</li><li>Slightly more expensive</li></ul>

	• Wood shavings do not stick to gloves	• Stiff during first uses • Makes hand warm
Steel wire gloves	• Inexpensive • Comfortable • Usable on either hand • Slightly cooler than other gloves	• Wood shavings stick to the gloves • Can puncture • Slightly more rigid • Frays with use
Metal mesh gloves	• Highly cut resistant • Durable • Feels safer	• Slightly less grip • Bit more uncomfortable • Expensive
Shop gloves	• Readily available • Affordable • Many colors and styles	• Mostly not cut-resistant • Can puncture easily • Not durable
Finger guards	• Affordable • Portable • Cooler to wear • Maintains dexterity	• Exposes other fingers and palms • Can puncture • Fit may be loose

The biggest danger during whittling is cutting yourself. Gear up with proper gloves to prevent nasty cunts and blisters. Some people wear gloves on both hands but it is fine if you only use a glove on the hand holding the wood. Maybe try a combination of a glove on one hand and finger guards on the other hand. Regardless of your choice, always look after yourself and be safe while whittling.

Your Hands as a Tool

Of course, we cannot forget about your hands! These are the most important tools for whittling. Protecting your hands by wearing gloves is a great starting point, but there are many other ways to look after your hands and keep them healthy. Always look after your hands because without them there is no option to create artworks.

Whittling can be demanding on your hands. The joints and tendons are getting quite the workout, especially at the start of your whittling journey. Luckily, there are several exercises to keep your hands strong. You might find your hands becoming even stronger by doing these exercises! Do these exercises often - before, during, and after whittling. You can even do them on days that you do not whittle.

The most basic exercise is making a fist and then opening your hands wide to stretch your fingers. Hold your hands in each position for about 30 seconds and repeat the exercise about five times. A variation of this exercise is to curl your fingers into a claw and then stretch the fingers open. Another alternative is to squeeze a soft ball or bean bag in each hand and hold this grip for 10 seconds before releasing the ball.

Another stretch helps in strengthening your palms and joints. Place the palm of your hand on a clean surface. While straightening your fingers, push your hand into the table lightly and hold this position for about 30 seconds. While your hand is in this flat position, proceed to another exercise by lifting one finger at a time into the air. Finish this exercise set by keeping your palm on the surface and lifting all your fingers at once.

Whittling often irritates the thumb and thumb joints. Flexing your thumb can ease some of the tension and improves your range of motion. Open your hand and hold it comfortably in front of you. Fold your thumb over your palm so that the tip of the thumb touches the bottom of your little finger. Hold this position for 30 seconds then open your thumb into a stretch. Repeat this exercise about five times and do it several times each day.

Exercising your hands is a fantastic way to keep them healthy. These exercises make your hands stronger and alleviate pain from overuse injuries. It also helps improve your range of motion and motor skills.

Ultimately, sore hands depend on the type of knife you choose for whittling. Purchasing a knife with an ergonomic handle is the best way to ensure comfort. Whittling places constant pressure on your hands and friction aggravates the problem, which may cause blisters. This situation is normal. Make your hands more comfortable by investing in thicker gloves, although it might decrease your grip on the wood.

Taking Care of Your Equipment

Taking care of your equipment is just as important as looking after your hands. Blunt knives are a nuisance to use and can aggravate injuries. Luckily, it is easy to maintain your whittling equipment. Your knife should be clean and dry. You can wash knives in warm water with mild detergent and dry it properly with a paper towel or microfiber cloth. Do not soak the knife or use a dishwasher and never use abrasive sponges or coarse clothes.

Sharpening your knives frequently makes them a pleasure to use. Use a honing rod, leather strop, or stone and make long strokes to sharpen the knife. Sharpening knives with machines and belts is not a good idea as the heat and excess abrasion often damage the steel, rendering your prized possession warped and unusable. Take your knives to a professional for a proper service and sharpening every year.

Knives made from carbon steel require additional care. Acids can harm a carbon steel blade, so wash the knife properly after every use. Use a cloth to apply a food-based oil over the blade to prevent corrosion.

Storing your knives is important for safety and to maintain the knife's integrity. Wrap your knife in a leather strip, place it back in its sheath or pouch, or get a magnetic strip to hold your knives when not in use.

I am sure you are eager to start whittling! So, keep your hands healthy through exercise, maintain your gear and update your equipment occasionally. Doing these things ensure you will be whittling for years to come!

Chapter 3:
Beginner-Level Techniques

Now, you could just grab your knife and start hacking away at any scrap of wood, but it's definitely not going to produce the best results. Your capabilities are far beyond some meager attempts! Before you start whittling, you should understand some techniques and know proper knife use for successful projects.

At this stage, you already respect your knives. This same respect should be visible when using your knives. Knowing how to properly whittle the wood you have chosen not only makes your life easier but generates a more efficient whittling process. Let's get into some basic cuts.

The Basic Whittling Cuts

There are several whittling techniques for beginners. Practice these cuts often and you will gain confidence soon enough. Start with the three basic cuts: straight rough cut, push stroke, and pull stroke. Afterwards, attempt the other techniques. Your cuts might not be perfect, but every additional stroke adds to your whittling experience.

Straight Rough Cut

The straight rough cut is the first cut used in any whittling project. Use it to create a rough outline of the object you are making. Sweep the knife along the grain of the wood and away from your body. The objective is to make long shallow cuts that remove unnecessary wood.

Push Stroke

The push stroke is another preparatory cut. Angle the knife and wood away from your body, then cut away large parts of the wood to reveal the basic elements of your design. Only cut away manageable segments and remember to cut along the grain. Some people try to take off a lot of wood at once and then cut into their design area, forcing them to restart the project. Be patient and rather remove smaller areas without hurting yourself or compromising the design.

Pull Stroke

The pull stroke is known as a paring cut. Think about this cut as the one you use when you peel a carrot or potato. Rest the thumb of your cutting hand against the end of the wood and pull the knife towards you. Always wear a thumb guard when making the paring cut as the knife often stops on your thumb. The pull stroke is perfect for creating details as you have more control over the knife.

Leveraging Cut

Sometimes called the thumb push, push-away, or push stroke, this cut is essential when creating the basic project shape. This cut is made away from your body with a controlled pushing motion. While holding the knife in your cutting hand, place the thumb of your other hand on the back of the knife's blade. The supporting hand pushes the blade to make the cut. Simultaneously, the hand holding the knife directs the blade to make smooth, precise cuts. The leveraging cut works well if the design has awkward shapes or if the position is too tight for paring strokes.

V-Cut

Have you ever wondered how whittlers get those thin lines resembling hair or grass in their designs? Well, the answer is the V-cut. A V-cut is a very thin cut that adds depth or grooves to your project. Start by deciding how deep and wide the cut should be. Next, holding your knife at an angle, cut into the wood. Remove the knife and change the angle slightly when making the next cut. If done correctly, the cuts line up beneath the wood. Remove the wood chips or shavings to reveal the v-shaped groove. Some whittlers call the V-cut a channel-cut since it creates channel shapes in the wood.

Techniques for Beginners

Before starting your project, get together your equipment. The most basic requirements are a knife, wood, and a whittling idea. However, some extra items will not go amiss. At various stages of the project, you may require a marker, cleaning cloth, sandpaper, and mineral oil. Let's get into some beginner techniques, which will show how you will use these items and work with wood.

Wood is a beautiful medium for artworks. The most important thing to remember is that wood has a grain. Always make your cuts along the grain as the knife will glide smoothly. Cutting across the grain is inevitable and suitable for whittling, although these cuts can be trickier to make. Never cut against the wood grain, as it leads to splintering, which ruins the wood and your blade.

A typical whittling project tends to follow certain steps. Once you decide on a design, draw it out on the wood using a pencil or marker. Start making straight rough cuts and push strokes to remove unnecessary wood segments. Next, use the leverage (thumb push) cut and pull stroke to whittle the finer details. These techniques work best for making curves and rounding edges. You might also use the V-cut for decorative elements or making grooves. Once your cutting is complete, sand the wood to create a smooth finish. Use sandpapers with different grits, such as 100, 150, and 220 grit. Wipe the piece down after every sanding. Finally, apply mineral oil to the wood using a clean cloth. Not all people sand and oil their work - it is a matter of personal preference.

Some projects have intricate designs and feature cut-out segments. Instead of grooves, you might want to cut a triangular or pyramid shape into the wood. This method is similar to the V-cut and easy to do. Let's say you want to cut a deep triangular shape into the wood and draw a triangle on the wood. Start making an angular cut along the edge of the first line. Gently apply more pressure to the blade while deepening the cut towards the middle of the line, then reduce the pressure as you reach the end of the line. Repeat this process with the other two sides. If all goes well, you should be able to remove a triangular chip from the wood.

Whittling is fun and easy, yet, frustration can set in when things do not go according to plan. Take a break when you get stuck. Sometimes, a few minutes away from the wood gives you time to think about where it might be going wrong. Come back to the project with a renewed mind and positive energy. Soon your project will be back on track!

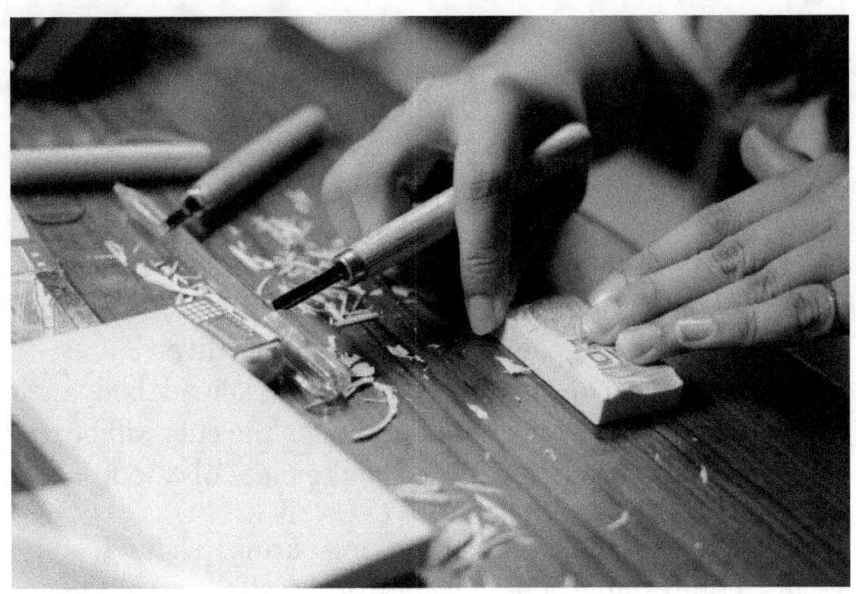

Plan Your Project

Whittling requires planning. Know what you want to achieve when you start a project, as it helps you understand the steps towards the end goal. You will know what to expect as you move through your project and start making plans if things go a little off course.

Start by selecting a piece of wood that is a reasonable size for your desired end product. Do not use a piece of wood that is too small or too large. Inappropriate sizes just waste your time. Also consider your design and whether it is suitable for a specific type of wood. It is better to find a project based on the wood you have available as it will flow better while whittling.

Having an end goal in mind provides direction to your whittling. A specific object or design maintains your focus and you constantly consider whether the next stroke will reveal the image. But remember, there is a big chance that you will "mess up" and that is okay. Just be patient. Simultaneously, be prepared to improvise and alter your design slightly.

Play-by-Play

Let's say your whittling project is a little standing bear. Most whittling projects come with measurements, so find a piece of wood that is the correct size to fit the given dimensions. Start by measuring out the ears, head, body with arms, and the feet. Think about how deep the cuts will be too - you can make markings all around the piece of wood.

Start defining the head by making paring, pushing, and V-cuts. For example, a paring cut works well to create the rounding of the head, while a V-cut combined with a thumb push stroke can help in defining the neck of the bear. Next, make rounded paring cuts for the basic foot shape. A V-cut works well in defining the arms and ears of the bear.

Focus on adding definition as you go through the process. Make the ears rounder, give the head a proper shape, and remove more wood from the upper torso to give the idea of a stomach. Remove wood shavings between the feet and body to give the illusion of legs. Finally, use thin V-cuts to create arm-bends, fingers, toes, and a snout. Draw eyes and a nose onto the wood to help you in whittling the finer features. You can keep them plain, or paint eyes and other facial features onto the bear.

Sharpening Your Knife

A sharp knife is safer and makes whittling easier. Sharp blades slide easier through the wood, so you do not need to apply as much pressure. Applying excessive pressure on the knife is an indicator of a dull blade and can slip quickly causing cuts to your hands. Sharpening your knives takes some time but it is not difficult.

Select the knives you want to sharpen and place them on a clean surface. Find a separate flat surface, such as acrylic board or glass, which is perfectly smooth. Apply adhesive spray to the surface and then stick sandpaper onto it. Wet and dry sandpaper with a 200 grit works well for the first sharpening. Place the cutting edge of the blade against the sandpaper and slide it across the paper. Use a light movement to push the blade away from your body and into the cutting edge at a slight angle. Flip the knife over and now run the other side of the cutting edge across the sandpaper.

Continue sharpening your knife by using additional grits of sandpaper. After using the 200-grit sandpaper, sharpen the blade against a 400 and 600-grit paper to smooth out any scratches. Finally, place the blade flat onto a piece of leather and slide the knife across it. Do not put it at an angle as it will cut the leather. Just polish the blade with the leather by sliding it forward using the dull end.

Now that your knives are sharp, you can start whittling with confidence. Take it easy when whittling. Move slowly - there is no rush. Have fun during the process! Whittling should be a positive experience, but prepare yourself for some hiccups along the way. Be mentally prepared for small cuts, slivers, and other irritants - knowing about these possibilities ahead of time means you won't get frustrated quickly. Pro tip: Remove slivers by placing duct tape over the area and then remove the tape gently pulling the sliver out with it.

Ensure the wood you select is dry before starting the project. Wet wood can warp or crack as it dries out, which can change your artwork entirely. Sometimes, the wood is too hard or too soft, which results in difficulty when creating intricate details. Apply a 50/50 mixture of water and rubbing alcohol to the wood, making it easier to work with. But, it is always better to just know your wood well!

Chapter 4:
The Wood You Choose Makes a Difference!

The wood you choose determines everything! Ultimately, wood is the only constant throughout your project. From start to finish, you will manipulate the same piece of wood. Your choice of wood is the most important part of this process. Heartwood is at the center of the tree and has different characteristics to the external sapwood. The best types of wood for carving and whittling fall into two categories: softwoods and hardwoods.

Softwood

The gymnosperm family of trees, including fir and pine, are called softwoods and usually reproduce through cones or nuts. Softwoods often have a sticky sap, so it is important to use dry wood. Softwoods are popular choices for the construction industry, producing paper pulp, manufacturing furniture, making chipboard, and woodturning. Softwoods are known for having a consistent thickness and density, which are valuable characteristics.

Softwoods are a popular choice for many reasons. They grow very quickly, so softwoods are inexpensive. It is easier to cut softwoods because there are fewer grain patterns. Softwood trees have a high resistance to insects, which make them a great option for items that should last a lifetime.

Unfortunately, there are some negatives to softwood. The wood has a low density, which makes it quite flammable if it is exposed to flames. This poor resistance to fire is the reason that softwoods do not make good firewood - they burn too quickly. Some softwoods are prone to decay and maintaining them can be a challenge if you do not look after your products consistently. The sticky sap is another issue that complicates carving, especially if the wood is still a bit wet.

Hardwood

Hardwood stems from angiosperm trees, which use flowers for reproduction. Hardwoods include oak, elm, and mahogany trees, among others. Pores of various sizes, dominant grains, and slower-growing are features of hardwoods, which often lose their leaves during autumn. Hardwood is used in building boats, cooking, construction, and musical instruments.

Hardwood has several desirable properties. It has a high density, which makes it easy to look after over the years. Generally, hardwood is fire and decay-resistant, but some pieces may fall prey to insect infestation. Ironically, the density of hardwood makes it a desirable option for use in campfires because it burns slowly.

There are disadvantages to hardwood. It is quite expensive because it takes so many years to grow. The more texture, growth rings, and detail a hardwood has, the more expensive it becomes. Hardwood is challenging to cut because of the grain and pores (small holes). Speaking of grain, let's have a better look at this distinguishing feature of wood.

Wood Grain

Most beginners choose softwood as it is easier to whittle. Softwood has fewer knots and the softness makes it ideal for smooth cutting strokes. Yet, when you are starting out with whittling, it is important to understand the grain of your wood.

Look at a large cut of any wood and you will see distinct rings. These rings are a growth record of the tree. A new ring is added with every growth cycle the tree grows through. These circles form the grain of the tree when it is cut.

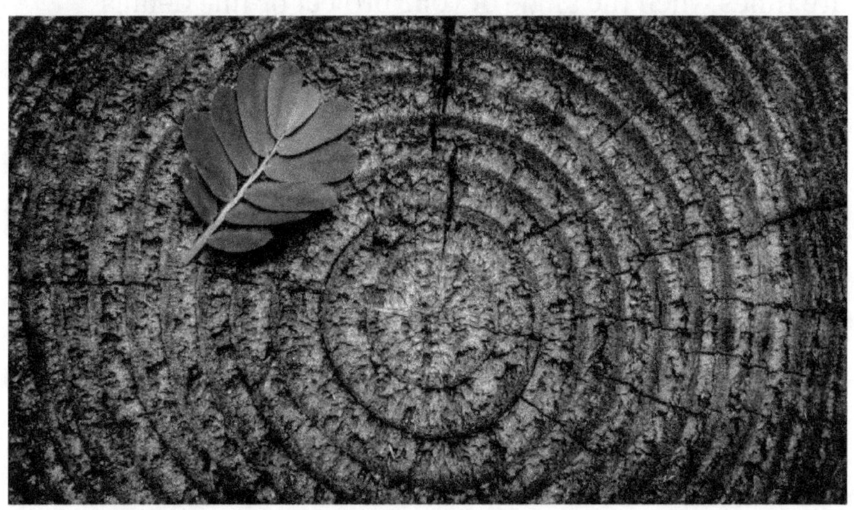

Grain dynamics describes the way the grain works with your knife. Cutting slivers of wood in the same direction as the grain is known as cutting along the grain and is easy to do. Think about when you pet an animal. If you stroke a dog's fur in the direction it grows, then it is smooth and your hand glides over it easily. This example is the same as cutting along the grain. However, if you move your hand in the opposite direction of your pet's hair, then it causes friction, sticks up, and makes it difficult to work with. The same happens if you cut against the grain of the wood.

Luckily, checking the grain direction is a simple process. Take your piece of wood and cut a sliver off from one end. A smoothly gliding knife indicates you are cutting with the grain. If your knife gets stuck or struggles to move through the wood, then you are cutting against the grain. Turn the block so that you can cut from the other direction - you should be cutting with the grain now.

Sometimes, you will have to cut against the grain. There are times when the angle of your project or fine details require cutting against the grain. This situation usually arises from tight spaces and not being able to turn the piece in a way that gives access to the grain. It should not be a problem though. Simply whittle like you normally would but keep your safety gear in place. Make your cuts smaller and increase the number of cuts to avoid wood splintering. For beginners, it is best to find a softwood with a straight grain and attempt projects that move with the grain.

Best Softwoods for Beginners

There are many softwoods to choose from, so how do you know which one is best? Well, learning more about each type of softwood makes your decision easier. If you know your wood, then you can determine the best type for each project. Besides considering the grain and softness, also think about the color you want from the final product. Luckily, all the designs in this book will guide you in the best wood choice for the task.

Basswood

Basswood is a favorite for beginner whittlers. The fine grain and softness make whittling easy. Some basswood pieces have very faint textures making them popular for carving intricate designs. The color of the wood is similar to cream with darker coloration around the edges. The inner bark is tough and fibrous, which works well for ropes and cords.

The basswood tree grows rapidly in moisture-rich upland slopes and woods. Some basswood trees are visible in ravines and bluffs if the surrounding landscape provides protection from the elements. Basswood trees easily adapt to different soil conditions, although they prefer proper drainage. However, basswood trees grow in both shade and full sun. It is native to Iowa and has the Latin name *Tilia americana*, although some people call it the American Linden tree. A fully grown basswood tree is between 75 and 130 feet in height. The lifespan of basswood is approximately 15 years, which is a short lifetime compared to other trees.

The leaves of the basswood tree create rich foliage and provide shade. So you might just find a piece of basswood and be able to whittle it underneath the tree! Leaves range in length from 3 - 6 inches and have a heart shape. The bark of the basswood has a silver-gray color, while the twigs start off light brown before turning gray. A dark red bud is visible at the end of twigs, so look out for these buds when identifying trees. During summer, the basswood boasts creamy yellow flowers and the fruit of the tree is nut-like stemming from a feathery open pod.

The biggest disadvantage of basswood is its poor resistance to decay. Specifically, the heartwood decays quickly once the tree reaches maturity, causing a hollow interior. Many birds and woodland animals create nests and homes in the cavities of basswood trees. Keep in mind that the flowers of basswood trees attract bees, so check the tree carefully before removing any wood.

Basswood has many uses, which make it popular among all people interested in wood. Beekeepers often plant basswood, as it attracts honey bees that produce honey with a distinct taste. Fruit and vegetable crates, Venetian blinds, and barrels frequently contain basswood. It also features in furniture as hidden slats. Of course, all wood carvers are familiar with basswood. Most beginners select basswood as it is the easiest to work with, relatively inexpensive, and available from most hardware and craft stores.

Balsa

Balsa is a type of softwood that most of us have come into contact with already. Most wooden toys, even those purchased in toy stores, are made from balsa. Also, it is a popular choice for making model aircraft and bridges. It features in radio-controlled vehicles and planes, which are used for participation in model aircraft competitions.

Balsa is a lightweight wood that is native to North and South America. It is part of the mallow family and its Latin name is *Ochroma pyramidale*. Although people plant these trees, they also appear naturally in agricultural fields and forest clearings. Balsa grows extremely quickly and often reaches heights of just under 100 feet within 15 years. The full lifespan of the tree is 30 to 40 years.

Balsa produces a distinct flower after the third year. Its flowers are large and deep with nectar attracting many species, including birds, capuchin monkeys, and bats. The large leaves grow up to 15 inches in length, which creates a beautiful evergreen tree producing lots of shade.

Its lightness, strength, and durability, make balsa worthwhile for many applications. Besides model aircraft, the de Havilland Mosquito plane in World War II contained balsa components. It also features in fishing lures and crankbaits, while some writers use balsa wood for calligraphy writing. Setmakers for stage and film productions use balsa to manufacture props. These props include breakaway furniture that breaks apart easily when a scene requires rage or frustration.

Balsa works well as part of composite materials used in manufacturing other things. Table tennis bats, wind turbines, and plywood frequently include balsa as the main component in their construction. The topsides of boats and entire surfboards may include balsa wood combined with fiberglass for extra strength. Chevrolet combined carbon fiber with balsa wood in manufacturing the floor pans for certain models of the Corvette.

The color is a deeper cream colour, which leans towards beige. It has a low density and is lighter than cork because of its rapid growth, but this is only the case once the wood dries. Living balsa wood is quite heavy because its cells contain water. These cells later produce a strong wood structure when empty and dry, making balsa a versatile option. Balsa is a great choice for whittling, especially to produce designs that require much shaping. Balsa wood is cheap and stocked in most craft supply and hardware stores.

Pine

Pine trees are a familiar sight in most parts of the world. The trees have many distinct characteristics including pine cones, needles, and leaves. Besides using the wood, pine cones often feature in decorations and props. Just think about combining a whittled deer or Santa with a pine cone Christmas tree! Pine trees have a familiar aroma that appeals to many people and even become fragrances purchased in stores.

Pine trees, part of the *Pinaceae* family, proliferate many parks and forests. These trees are evergreens with most reaching heights of 50 to 150 feet, although some pine trees grow up to 260 feet tall. Unlike some of the other softwoods, pine trees grow for decades. The branches on a pine tree form a continuous spiral, similar to the Fibonacci sequence. New branches have a whitish-brown color and point upwards, which led to these new sections being called candles.

The bark of pine trees is scaly and thick, although some variations have flaky and thin bark. Four leaf types make the pine tree unique as it has seeds, juvenile leaves, scale leaves, and finally, needles. About two to seven needles are found in each cluster, which lives for 18 months to 40 years. Pine cones feature scales with female cones reaching up to 23 inches, while males only grow to 2 inches in length. There are numerous types of pine trees based on pollination, soil conditions, and climate. Wind pollination, lengthy lifetimes, and human interference resulted in hybrid pine species with each having unique characteristics.

Pinewood is versatile, strong, and used in several industries. A favorite among lumberjacks, pine is one of the first choices in building log cabins, window frames, and roofs, and floors. A lot of furniture is made from pine wood and it takes on paint or color stain, so you can personalize it if you do not want to see the plain wood. The light-weight of pine makes it easy to move around, so even large doors are made from pine. Some paper products come from pine wood, while also being a popular addition to composite materials.

The longer life span of pine trees produces more defined grains, which makes carving slightly more difficult. The coarser grain works well for whittling, but be patient and make shallower strokes. Pinewood comes in both off-white and yellowish tones, so the colour often makes it a great choice for natural artworks. Pine is readily available and reasonably priced, so give it a go after practicing on other softwoods.

Butternut

The butternut tree, also known as a white walnut tree or *Juglans cinerea*, is a type of walnut tree. It is found mostly in the east of the United States and parts of Canada. It is abundant in regions where it occurs naturally but requires soil with good drainage. Butternut is an evergreen tree but it has become endangered in some areas. Always ensure that the wood you cut or purchase is sourced sustainably and does not harm the flora population. In previous centuries, the bark of the tree was boiled to extract color for dying cloth. This color ranged from yellow to dark orange.

Butternut grows slowly, reaching heights of up to 130 feet. Most butternut trees are about 66 feet tall at maturity with a stem diameter of 16 to 31 inches. The leaves, consisting of several leaflets, can grow as long as 28 inches and have a yellow-green color. The flowers on a butternut tree are a light pink color and spiky. Its fruit is a nut, similar in shape to a lemon, with a green husk. A major obstacle for butternut trees is larger species that grow higher. Butternut cannot thrive in the shade and often deteriorate quickly in areas with competition for sunlight. They grow best in full sun with spacing between the trees.

This lightweight wood is ideal for carving and making furniture. It has more texture but cutting it along the grain allows for easy working. Butternut has a darker color and any piece of wood may contain several hues from beige to a deep caramel. This proliferation of color makes butternut a great choice for furniture, picture frames, and window frames. Applying a light oil brings the colors out more. It has a high resistance against rot, which makes it suitable for manufacturing objects that must last a long time.

Butternut is a softwood but it is trickier to work with. Butternut comes in rich caramel hues with lots of color variation, which makes it ideal for artworks. The coarse grain makes it chip easily, so be patient when using butternut. Some people prefer butternut for carving large items, but it works well for smaller whittling projects too. Unfortunately, butternut is not widely available. You may need to visit a timber store or lumberyard if you want a proper piece of butternut. Save some extra cash for your purchase, as butternut is a bit more expensive due to its scarcity.

Branches and Twigs

Most of us probably start our whittling journey by picking up a random piece of wood while out for a walk. Personally, I love walking around the forest and looking for interesting twigs or even fallen branches to whittle. One of the first cuts I practiced without any formal training was the straight rough cut. I would pick up twigs and make long strokes to remove the bark, slowly sharpening the tip of the twig into a pencil-like point. I am sure most of you had a similar experience with your own pocket knife.

Twigs and younger branches are softwoods. It does not matter what type of tree the wood comes from since twigs and branches are younger and have less grain. Twigs picked up are probably drying out already but you may need to leave some pieces to dry further before you start whittling. The size of the twig or branch also determines the type of designs you can whittle, so do not attempt anything too big.

The types and sizes of twigs and branches available depend on the location you are visiting. Ancient forests and woods may have larger pieces available, while the neighborhood park has younger trees and smaller pieces. Take your time when searching for twigs and branches. A pro tip is to take a carrier bag with you so that you can collect several pieces of suitable wood. Maybe you already have a project in mind. If it is the case, then search for a piece that fits your measurements well.

Moving to Hardwoods

Moving to whittling hardwoods early on is possible. Just make sure that you are very patient. Working with hardwood requires significantly more cuts and a shallower stroke. Be prepared for less precise movements of the blade. Start with a simple design and move to complicated projects once you have some experience and feel for hardwoods.

As you transition from softwoods to hardwoods, you might wonder which ones are the best to try. Cedar is a good option as it has similar characteristics to pine wood. It is a popular choice for storage containers, wardrobes, and roof shingles. Some music instruments use cedar wood in their construction because it is stable and lightweight. An alternative hardwood is aspen. Aspen trees are found in large quantities, which make them an asset to the timber industry. It is a lightweight wood that does not burn quickly. Matches, toothpicks, chipboard, and wood paneling all contain aspen wood. Even the beavers prefer aspen for constructing dams.

Black walnut and black cherry wood are suitable for more advanced whittlers. Black walnut wood has a compact grain, is hard, and has a high density. It is dark chocolate in color but polishing it reveals creamy beige areas from the sapwood. Flooring, furniture, and kitchen accessories can be made from black walnut. Black cherry has a relatively straight grain and random pores. The main disadvantage of black cherry is allergies to the sawdust appearing in many people. Black cherry has a distinct red hue spread throughout the heartwood, while the sapwood tends to yellow. These color variations make black cherry wood a preferred choice for cabinetry, woodturning, and flooring.

Remember that wood stumps and sheets are large, which may not be suitable for whittling. Craft stores sell wood blocks in different sizes, so choose the best one for your project. If you do cut your own wood, then you may need power tools to cut the wood into smaller segments for use in whittling.

Now that you know your wood, are you excited to start your first few artworks? Select some wood pieces that you feel comfortable working with and have a look at the projects in the next chapter. Ready, set, whittle!

Chapter 5: Basic Designs To Start Whittling

Whittling is a craft that requires practice and patience. Seeing your vision emerge from the wood creates excitement! There are so many beginner projects begging for your attention. Each design has a time indicator but remember to work at your own pace. You are still learning, so taking longer is fine. If your project does take its own direction, then follow the instructions to the best of your ability. Alternatively, continue with your own design since there is no right or wrong in whittling. Start by trying one of the following designs.

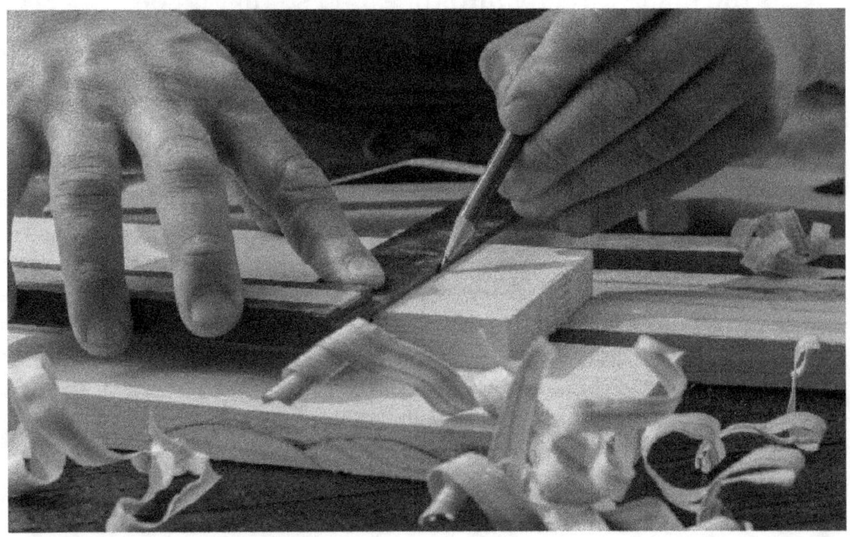

Whittled Whistle

A whistle is quick and easy to make. Any stick will work but select one that has its bark in good condition. There should be no cracks or missing pieces. The stick should be at least 4" in length and ⅓" wide. This quick project can be made in less than 15 minutes but with practice you can finish it in 5 minutes.

Instructions

1. Cut the end of the stick that you will put in your mouth at an angle and smooth it off so that you do not hurt yourself.

2. Use the V-cut to make a shallow notch about 1 ½" from the end of the stick. The first cut can be upright and the joining second cut at an angle. Remove the wood chip from the notch.

3. Move your knife about 1 ½" up from the notch. Press the blade directly into the wood so that it goes through the bark. Cut all around the stick to create a ring.

4. Wrap your hand around the bark under the cut ring area that includes the notch and gently twist to loosen the bark from the heartwood. Pull the bark off and keep it in a safe spot.

5. Using a paring cut, carve the notch deeper and longer. Keep the front edge in place but deepen it halfway into the stick. Lengthen the notch by a ½".

6. Use a push stroke to remove long wood shavings from the notch towards the mouth edge, so that the stick has a flat area on the top.

7. Replace the bark back over the stick and line up the notch area. Your whistle is ready for use!

Owl Bookmark

Sometimes you want a quick whittling project using twigs or branches. Any stick works for this project but get one that is at least ½" thick and free of knots, otherwise, it might become difficult to add detail. Remember that all twigs and branches are soft and have little grain, so you can choose one to your liking. Cut it to about 6". This bookmark takes as little as 10 minutes to whittle making it a great option if you just need a quick break. Any pocket knife works but you might want a raindrop razor edge if you plan on adding fine details.

Instructions

1. Split your stick into quarters lengthwise. The best way to get enough force is to place the stick upright with your blade resting on top of it. Do not lock your blade into place; just hold it with one hand. Then, take another stick and tap the blade from the top, giving it enough force to slide through the stick.

2. Use one of the quarters as a stick. Make a shallow cut about 1" from the top along the exposed wood. Next, use paring strokes to smooth the wood in the top 1" and round the corner slightly.

3. Make a shallow "x" cut within the first third of the clean area. It should cross on the corner and extend to the top corner of each side, forming two triangles. Remove the wood in each triangle until they are about ⅛" deep. Make each triangle slightly rounder for eyes

4. Using V-cuts accentuate the x-shape. From the inverted "v" at the bottom of the eyes, round out the body towards the bottom of the stick.

5. Cut a "v" into the top of the stick and parallel to the top of the "x". Remove this wood ship entirely, revealing the eyebrows of the owl.

6. Using the cut made in step 2 as a marker, start removing the excess wood below the owl using leverage cuts. You want to create a flat stick that fits into a book, so remove as much as necessary. Also, remove the bark at the back of the stick and flatten this side by cutting the wood away until you are left with a flat bookmark.

Maori Hook Pendant

The fish hook pendant is worn by Maoris but became popular in the film Moana. This fast whittling project makes a simple necklace when tied to leather yarn. These pendants come in different sizes although they usually measure about 2" in length and 1" in width. It is approximately ⅓" thick. Use a softwood such as basswood or balsa for this design, as you will probably cut against the grain at some point. Yet, these little pendants look great in other types of wood too, especially with distinctive coloration. Alternatively, find a stick or branch in nature and use that for your pendant. Keep in mind that you would have to whittle the stick down to a block before you can begin. The curves in this design are a bit tricky as the space is tight. Use a raindrop razor edge blade and set aside about 15 minutes.

Instructions

1. Draw a hook onto the plank. It is an open circle with a segment extending a little further up to hold the yarn.

2. Use thumb push strokes to cut away excess wood around the outside of the design. Leave a piece of wood attached to the bottom of the hook, which will be used later for the fin design.

3. Carefully remove the wood on the inside of the design by using V-cuts.

4. Shape the fishtail by making a shallow V-cut into the end of the hook. Also, carve a distinct "v" into each side of the hook just before the curve turning towards the end. You want it to look like a fishtail with the hook becoming thinner before reaching the tail.

5. Using paring strokes, remove all square edges around the design to give a round shape.

6. Turn your attention to the wood at the bottom of the hook. Make a small V-cut into the section facing the extending side of the hook, creating a fin. Then, define the fin by removing all the extra wood so that only the hook remains.

7. Using V-cuts, make a channel around the pendant about ⅓" from the top of the extending piece.

8. Sand the pendant till smooth. Tightly wrap a long piece of leather string around the channel several times and tie the lengths together to form the necklace.

Boomerang

For this boomerang, you can use a precut wood slab or find a branch with a natural elbow bend. Harder wood is preferable because it won't break easily if the boomerang lands awkwardly. Black walnut or black cherry is a stunning choice if you want the natural grain and colors to shine through. If you use a branch, then you have to cut it smaller using an electric saw and let the wood dry. The instructions below assume you have a slab measuring 22" x 9" x ⅓" but you can adapt it easily to the cut branch. This project uses basic techniques and takes about 45 minutes to make. A pocket knife is the only tool you need, although a hook knife is handy too.

Instructions

1. Draw a boomerang onto the wood board. Find the middle of the board at the top and make a curve, then make another curve about one inch below the first. Also, make half circles in the bottom left and right corners. Connect the curves to create the boomerang shape. Usually, the boomerang widens towards the edges of the wings and is thinner near the middle.

2. Cut the boomerang along the outline using straight rough cuts.

3. Once you have the basic shape, use thumb push strokes to define the lines.

4. Use paring cuts to accentuate the curves and round all the edges on the longer lengths of the boomerang.

5. The concave (inner) section of the elbow is trickier to smooth out but a hook knife can make the task easier.

6. Sand and oil the boomerang, then fling it through the air and see it travel!

Chess Pawn

Chess pieces are a popular project for many whittlers. You can create any design you want for your chess pieces. This pawn design follows the traditional style. Find a stick about 1 ½" in diameter and at least 2" long. A longer stick is easier to work with because you can hold onto it while whittling the pawn. A simple pocket knife is all you need for this carving that uses all the basic whittling skills. This project takes about 30 minutes.

Instructions

1. Remove the bark using straight rough cuts.

2. Start making the head of the pawn by rounding off the top of the stick using push cuts. The top of the stick should be entirely round.

3. Draw a line all around the stick about ¾" from the top. Rock your knife back and forth over this line to make an indentation in the wood. Make a small notch from the head's side towards this line to create a groove. Use paring cuts to then round out the bottom of the head towards the indented line. Essentially, you want a ball shape for the top of the pawn.

4. Make another deeper indented line ¼" below the first one for the collar of the pawn.

5. Next work from the bottom of your stick towards the collar. If your stick is longer then you want to mark a

line around the stick, approximately 1" below the
collar.

6. Working carefully, use push cuts to remove the wood
    from the bottom of the pawn to the collar. You want
    the "body" section beneath the collar to be thin and
    then flare it out towards the bottom. Deepen the
    bottom collar line as you remove the excess wood.

7. Cut off excess wood at the bottom of the piece, if
    necessary. Sand your pawn and apply oil or give it a
    coat of paint.

Spiral Pencil

Most of us have a pencil lying around the house. A
wooden pencil is something you can use to practice fine
whittling designs. Choose a pencil that is round for this
project. Once you are comfortable with whittling a round
pencil, you can move on to six-sided pencils. The wood used
for pencils varies so prepare yourself for some unexpected
obstacles in the process. The biggest issue may be the grain,
as this design inevitably cuts across and against the grain at
times. A pocket knife or raindrop razor edge is a good option
but make sure the blade is sharp. This project takes about 30
minutes with some practice. Although, taking your time with
this design is a sound strategy as it is a technique that you
need to master.

Instructions

1. Start at the blunt edge of the pencil. Using a thumb
    push stroke, make two thin cuts parallel to each other.

2. Place your knife into the first cut and continue cutting
    all around the pencil right to the sharp tip. It should

create a spiralized line. Do the same thing with the
second thin cut you made in the first step.

3. Starting at the blunt end of the pencil, use a V-cut to
    whittle out the area between the two initial cuts.
    Create the groove by cutting into the middle of the
    wood at an angle from the first line, then cut at an
    opposite angle from the second line. Make the groove
    all around the length of the pencil.

4. Use the tip of your knife to remove any rough or
    inconsistent edges within the spiral cut-out.

5. Fold some sandpaper into a small point and gently
    sand the grooves within the spiral.

The pencil might not be usable anymore, but at least you
have had good practice whittling at all angles and making
fine cuts. Dip it in some paint and add a thin string to it, then
hang it in a window. The colors and shape make it
interesting to look at as it twirls in the wind.

Letter Opener

A hand-carved letter opener is a special gift. Use any
type of stick for this project but make sure most of the bark is
still intact, especially at the handle section. Find a piece that
is 1" thick and at least 8" in length. It is okay if the stick has a
slight curve in it. Try to stick with pine or butternut. A pocket
knife and 30 minutes are what you need for this project.

Instructions

1. Cut a line ⅛" below one end of the stick. Make a
    notch from this line and round it towards the edge.
    This side is the handle part.

2. Make another cut line ⅓" from the first line and create a groove using V-cuts.

3. Make the next cut line 2 ½" from the end of the handle to the front and create a slightly wider and deeper groove along this line.

4. A final line should be made 3" from the end of the handle towards the front.

5. Turn the stick around so that the blade end is available. Starting about 5" back, make long rough cuts to get a flat section. Repeat it on the other side so that both sides of the blade are flat. You want it to be about ⅛" in thickness.

6. Turn the wood so that you can work on the thin edge of the blade. From your starting point use a rough cut to remove the bark and thin out the blade towards the front. Do the same on the other side of the thin blade.

7. Carve a notch between the handle and blade using the cut line as a guide. You want the letter opener to be thinner in this neck area. Work on creating a shallow groove in this section.

8. Work with the tip of the blade area. Shape it to form a gradual sharp point. Bevel all edges of the blade into thinner areas.

9. Use a fine-grit sandpaper to smooth any rough areas on the blade. Add some oil to protect the letter opener. You can add further decorative details to the handle, like spirals or notches.

Tiny Guitar

Most whittlers also enjoy their music and play instruments. This teeny-tiny guitar is a fun project that taps into both these hobbies. It is very small but you can scale it for large wood pieces too. Use softwood blocks, specifically balsa with its creamy color, for this design. A 2" x 1" x ½" piece of wood works best, but you can use a twig or branch and cut it to this size too. The smoothest results come from a flat steel blade. Leave yourself at least 30 minutes for this design as the size makes it slightly more difficult to whittle.

Instructions

1. Draw a guitar onto the wood. Start at the top of the length and draw a neck in the middle - two lines about ¼" apart that taper slightly from top to bottom. Add a simple triangle at the top of the neck to give an illusion of the tuning section. Then draw the body of the guitar over the rest of the block. It is the number "8" but keep the top loop smaller than the bottom one. Round out the middle of the body to make cutting easier. Extend the neck slightly into the body (about ⅓"). Draw a rectangle in the bottom section of the body.

2. Cut out the blind using thumb push strokes and paring cuts. Be careful when whittling around the neck as any slip of the knife may remove it entirely.

3. Make an indented cutting line around the neck area where it enters the face of the body and add indented cuts around the rectangle. Draw a straight line from this neck area to the rectangle below. Remove an ⅛" layer of wood from the face of the guitar but leave the

raised areas for the rectangle and neck of the guitar. Use paring cuts or thumb push strokes while whittling this section.

4. Draw a small circle in the middle of the body, between the neck and the rectangle. Now, carefully use the tip of your knife to hollow out a small hole, or take the lazy way out and drill a shallow hole.

5. Sand the entire guitar, ensuring you get into all the corners.

Ball in a Cage

Whittlers always try to push their boundaries with new designs and this is one of those projects that leave others in awe. The ball in a cage is a fun design as you carve both the cage and ball at the same time from one block of wood. It takes quite some time, so set aside at least two hours. Spend enough time on marking out all sides of the wood with the design, as it will make or break the final product. Balsa or basswood is advised for this project as you will be carving against the grain at some point. Start with a blank block measuring 3" x 1" x 1". Get into all corners and produce roundings by using a raindrop razor edge knife.

Instructions

1. Draw a line ⅓" from all sides of the wood to produce a rectangle. You should mark out every single side of the wood because you are carving on all sides.

2. Measure out ⅔" from the short line of the rectangle and draw another line perpendicular to the longer side. Repeat this step from the other short line too. You should now see a rectangle divided into three

parts with the middle section being the largest. Repeat this process on the other three sides with rectangular frames.

3. Make a cutting line with your knife on all of the penciled lines. You can use a V-cut to widen the line slightly, but keep it as thin as possible.

4. Begin removing wood from each of the smaller rectangles. Start on one side and work your way around. The aim is to hollow out these rectangles by about ⅓". Keep moving from one rectangle to the next, especially if you feel stuck on a specific side.

5. Next, focus on the ball in the middle. Start by cutting a bevel towards each side of the cage on all the different faces of the block. Use thumb push strokes for this part as it is a bit tight to manage paring cuts. Start to form the ball shape, although it will probably look like an ellipse at this stage. Work on the top half first, and whittle it into a roundish shape. As you do so, the remaining wood left in the top part of the cage should start to become less and eventually leave an opening that you can see through. Repeat the entire process with the bottom part of the ball.

6. Spend some time on refining your cage by shaving away any rough or inconsistent edges and flattening all surfaces.

7. Pay specific attention to the ball and focus on getting it as round as possible. Remember that it is sitting within the cage so make it slightly smaller than the frame around it. Continue this process until the ball comes loose from the frame entirely. You want it to

roll around in the frame. Get the shape as close to round as possible before releasing the ball from the wood holding it, otherwise, you are going to have trouble with holding the ball while whittling. Use thumb push strokes to form the roundings but keep your knife sharp. A dull knife will slip and cause damage to other parts of the structure.

8. The cage has a very angular shape. Refine the lines on the inside of the cage by shaving wood off in long strokes to create beveled bars. Do this with all the bars. You can round them off entirely if you prefer that look.

9. Sand the outside of the cage and parts you can get to as well as possible.

Ornamental Trivet

An ornamental trivet cis what many of us know as a potholder. It is a thick plate to put hot pots or casseroles on so that your table does not get heat damage. This design focuses on curves, circles, and swirls. It is great practice for rounding edges and using a hook knife. Turn this trivet into a drinks tray by adding handles onto the base. Butternut and pine work best for this design as it is hard enough to withstand heat but soft enough to carve curves. Use a 1" thick square board with a length and width of just over 10". You can make the trivet smaller or larger if you want, but keep the board thick for its purpose. Depending on the complexity of your design, this trivet takes upwards of 90 minutes to complete.

Instructions

1. Using a compass, draw a large circle with a 5" radius on the wood. Draw a second concentric circle with a radius of 4 ⅔". Now draw circles, swirls, and ovals on the wood, leaving at least ½" between each shape.

2. With a pocket knife, whittle around the outside circle so that you create the circular shape. Cut off any unnecessary corners and get the shape as close to a circle as possible.

3. Use the razor raindrop edge to cut into the interior circle. This cut is to give an interesting detail to the trivet. Run the knife over this line until it is about ⅕" deep.

4. Start with one of the shapes you drew on the inside and cut on the edge of the shape. You can accentuate the shape by making a V-cut to create a grooved edge going about ¼" deep.

5. For the next shape, cut on the shape outline. Next, use your hook knife to hollow out this shape. Repeat step 4 or 5 with the rest of the shapes you have drawn.

6. Use your pocket knife to round the edges of the trivet, making it easy to carry around.

7. Finish the trivet by sanding it until smooth and adding oil to protect the wood.

Flower Coasters

A whittled, homemade coaster set is a special gift for a friend or family member. Make four or six pieces for each set and give it away or sell them for a profit. The colors of butternut wood make it a beautiful choice for coasters, but you can use cedar or aspen if you want more vibrant colors. The usual coaster size is 4" x 4" x ¼". A raindrop razor edge and hook knife are best for this project. Each coaster takes about 30 minutes to whittle, so make one each day and you have a set by the end of the week!

Instructions

1. Sand the coaster to ensure the surface is flat before starting your design.

2. Draw a flower in the middle of the coaster. You can do this by making a circle (called the pistil) in the middle, then add five or six petals around the circle. For this project, make the body of the petal wide and let the tip of the petal end in a sharp point. Draw a line from the circle through the middle of each petal but let it stop before reaching the tip.

3. Use the raindrop razor edge knife to make a thin V-cut on the drawn circle. Also cut on both sides of the lines going through the middle of each petal.

4. Start whittling the petals by using the hook knife to cut from the outer edge of the petal up to the line in the middle of the petal. Then, cut the other side of the petal to the middle. Do not remove the thin line of wood in the middle of each petal. Use the raindrop razor edge to clean up the tips of the petals.

5. Add texture to the pistil by making small cuts into the circle. It should create fine lines.

6. Carefully sand into the petals and over the center until there are no rough spots. Add some dark stain to change the color, if you want. Otherwise, apply mineral oil with a soft cloth.

Wooden Knife

Why not make a knife with your whittling knife! A harder wood like aspen or cedar is suitable, although butternut and pinewood can work well. Any reasonably sized wood offcut will work - just remember that the size of the wood determines the final size of the knife. I suggest using a piece that is at least ½" thick, 5" long, and 1 ½-2" wide. A piece of wood that tapers to one end or becomes thinner is great too. You want a thicker edge to improve the grasp on the handle but the blade is thinner. This project takes about 20 minutes. Additionally, you need some leather twine, sandpaper, and wood glue for this design. A normal pocket knife or razor edge is best for this project.

Instructions

1. Decide which part of the wood will be the tip of the knife. Measure about three-fifths along the length of the wood and mark it all around. The longer section is the blade.

2. Whittle away any harsh corners on the handle area. Smooth the edges using paring cuts and cut a ring into the wood where the handle and blade meet.

3. Whittle the blade using rough cuts and push strokes. Focus on making the blade thinner on one side, which is the cutting edge. Also, cut the tip into a sharp point.

The cutting edge should be as thin as possible for cutting and have a good bevel (angle) for cutting.

4. Use an 80 grit sandpaper and sand with the grain to smooth out the blade. At the same time, you are sharpening the blade too. Move to finer sandpaper as you go along.

5. Finally, wrap leather twine around the handle to make it comfortable and use the super glue to hold it in place.

Spatula

A spatula has a basic design and is perfect to practice the basic whittling cuts. This design uses a piece of basswood or pine measuring 12"x 3 ½" x ½" but you can make a smaller or larger spatula if you like. A pocket knife is all you need for this design. It takes about half an hour to make a spatula

Instructions

1. Use a marker to draw the shape of your spatula onto the wood. A spatula has a rectangular shape attached to a thin handle, so draw the entire thing. The rectangle can be 3 ½" wide (the current block measurements) and about 4" in height. Now draw the handle along the middle of the wood block from the rectangle with measurements of 8" by ½". It is advisable to draw slightly rounded corners at the ends of the spatula and where the handle meets the rectangle. It gives a more polished look.

2. Using your pocket knife, remove excess wood around the drawn handle with rough straights. Do not worry about the squareness of the current handle, you will

make it rounder later on. The main focus now is
cutting the outline so that you can get the basic shape.
This cut-out basis shape is called a blank.

3. Using the paring stroke or thumb push cut, carve out
    the corners of the handle where it meets the spatula's
    rectangle. Soften all the corners on the spatula by
    gently removing a little bit of wood at a time so that
    there are no sharp edges.

4. Next, smooth out all sides of the spatula and handle
    by making paring cuts to create round edges. At this
    stage, you may want to whittle the rectangular shape
    in long strokes so that it becomes thinner towards the
    edge, which makes it easier to use.

5. Use sandpaper to smooth the wood and apply food-
    safe mineral oil. The spatula is ready for use in the
    kitchen.

Mixing Spoon

A mixing spoon is an essential kitchen utensil for mixing
batters, sauces, and even salads. It would be a great
handmade gift for any cook in your life. Mixing spoons come
in various sizes, so select a block of wood that works for you.
Although softwoods are best for beginners, this project is
easy enough to try your hand at cedar or aspen wood. You
will need a pocket knife and hook knife for this design.
Whittling the concave head of the spoon takes some time, so
set aside at least an hour for this design. Start with a wood
block measuring 10" x 3" x 1".

Instructions

1. Draw the basic shape of the spoon onto the wood. You may want to draw on the side of the wood too, as it gives a better view of the depth. The head of the spoon is round, so draw a circular shape attached to the handle. Make the head about 3" in diameter. Now draw the handle along the middle of the wood block from the circle with measurements of 7" by ½".

2. Using your pocket knife, remove excess wood around the outline with rough straight cuts. Shape the handle so that there are no square edges - all the corners should be round and the handle must be thin enough to hold comfortably. Shave the wood using a thumb push stroke to make the handle thinner where it reaches the head.

3. Turn the spoon so that the back (convex) side of the head is facing you. Use paring cuts to create a round shape to the head. Make sure the transition from the middle back of the head to the walls of the spoon are equal and smooth. You are aiming for a continuous slope around the head of the spoon.

4. Now for the front of the head, you want to create a concave shape similar to a bowl. Using your hook knife, start in the middle of the head and whittle out a small divot. Continue to make this bowl shape by working your way around the initial divot and going wider towards the rim of the spoon. You can decide how deep and wide the bowl must be; just ensure that it is uniform all around.

5. Smooth any rough edges on the entire object with your knife then start sanding the spoon until it is smooth and usable. Wipe it with food-safe oil and it is ready for use.

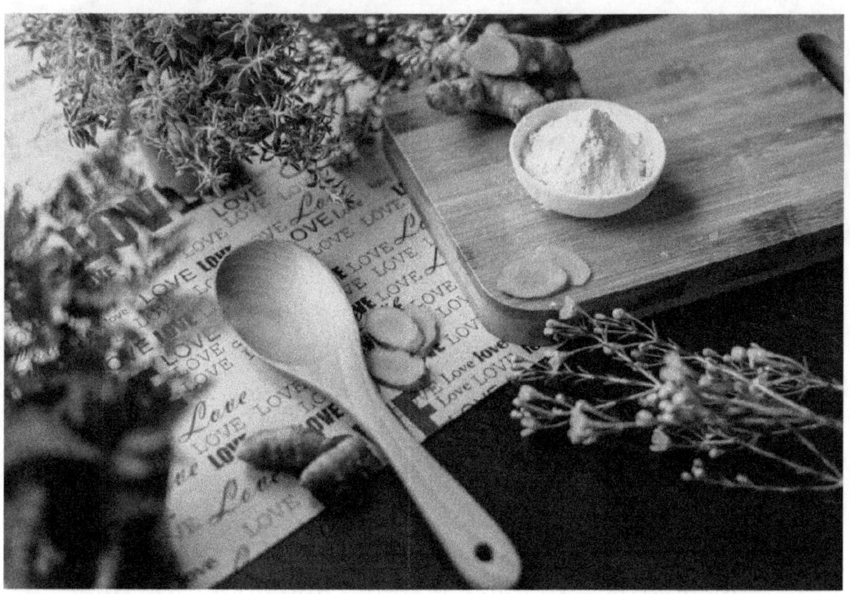

Salad Fork

A salad fork is the same thing as a normal fork just much larger. It helps in scooping salad out of a bowl. Use it with the mixing spoon to clamp the salad and transfer it easily to a plate. This salad fork has four prongs but you can make three or five depending on your preferences, and you can make them longer or shorter too. Most of your time will be spent carving the wood out between the prongs and getting the bevel just right. We will use similar sizes as the mixing spoon so that you can use them as a set. Remember that you can resize both of these utensils at any time for normal eating purposes. Use any softwood for this project but avoid pieces with many knots. Choose a straight grain segment measuring 10" x 3" x 1". This design easily takes two hours while using both a flat steel blade and hook knife with a wide diameter.

Instructions

1. Draw a basic fork shape onto the wood. The head of the fork curves in ever so slightly at the tip of the prongs, so draw an elliptical shape attached to the handle. Make the fork about 3" in width. Do not worry about drawing the prongs at this stage. Add a handle from the base of the fork and extend it to the end of the block so that it measures about 7" by ½". Smooth the connection between the head and handle by drawing in slight curves.

2. Use straight rough cuts to remove the wood around the outline with a flat steel blade.

3. Now concentrate on shaping the handle. Use thumb push strokes to make it round and about ½" thick. Make the handle a bit thinner as it reaches the head of the fork and focus on the curved base.

4. Work on the back of the fork's head. Use a thumb push stroke to create a slightly convex shape of the head. Ensure the transition between the middle and sides is equal. You want the entire head to have the same slope - it should not be as round as a spoon. Curve it slightly towards the base but keep the prong area straight.

5. Turn the fork so that you can work on the front of the head. Round out the base of the fork by using your hook knife and continue these strokes with the flat

steel blade over the prongs section. The prong area should be flat and have equal thickness throughout.

6. Now draw four prongs onto the head of the fork. Make each prong about 1" long and ⅛" wide. Using your flat steel blade cut an indentation line onto each prong line. Carve out the area between each prong by using V-cuts until you can fit the knife in for paring strokes. You can bevel the sides of each prong if preferred.

7. Sand the entire fork to remove any rough edges. It helps to fold the sandpaper in half when working between the prongs. Use a food-safe oil and soft cloth to treat the wood.

Bowl

This bowl is a larger whittling item but that does not mean it is complicated. In fact, it is the perfect project for trying out hardwoods since most of the design requires long thumb push strokes with the grain. Make it any size or depth you like. Maybe try this bowl as a set with the spoon and for above. Although you can use a thick branch or stump for this bowl, I would suggest using a pre-cut slab of wood to make your carving work less. Get a 15" x 12" x 4" slab of cedar or aspen. You want to use a wide-diameter hook knife for this project, as well as a pocket knife. This bowl takes a bit more time so schedule at least two hours, although it can take longer if the wood is very hard.

Instructions

1. With the large wood slab area facing upwards, draw a line 1" from each of the shorter sides. The section in the middle should measure 13" in length. Draw a large

elliptical shape within this rectangle. This ellipse is the outer rim of the bowl. Find the middle point of the 1" sections and draw a rectangle measuring 7" x 1". Now create a curve in each 7" section so that it links up with the bowl's outer rim. These 7" sections are the handles.

2. Turn the slab around. Find the midpoint of the slab to help you center your design. Draw a rectangle measuring 7" x 6" and then use this rectangle to draw another ellipse. This ellipse is the flat bottom of the bowl.

3. Turn the bowl back to the other side. Using your pocket knife, start shaving away sections around the bowl's outline until you are left with a blank. Straight rough cuts and push cuts work best.

4. Turn the wood around so that you can work on the convex side next. Using thumb push strokes, move your knife from the smaller ellipse to the rim of the bowl until you have a uniform inverted bowl shape. Remember to remove extra wood underneath the handles so that you can grip the bowl properly. Make the handles about ½" thick by using a combination of V-cuts for definition and thumb push cuts for wood removal.

5. Now turn the bowl to work on the inside. Take your hook knife and make a divot in the middle of the bowl. Work from the divot outwards using thumb push strokes to hollow out the bowl. You want the walls of the bowl to be a ½" thick. This section will take time, so be patient.

6. Work along the rim and handles. Use paring cuts to shave away the edges, leaving a rounded bevel-type edge.

7. Sand the entire bowl to make it smooth then apply a food-safe oil for wood protection.

Pizza Wheel Handle

Pizza - what a delicious treat! A pizza wheel slices through pizza with ease, so why not make one yourself. These instructions are for the handle. The blade for the wheel is made from metal, so you will need to purchase one or repurpose one you have at home. You also need a small screw and washer to secure the wheel to the handle. Use a pocket knife and hook knife for this design. Start with a block of pine or butternut wood measuring 5" x ¾" x ¾". This project takes about 45 minutes to make.

Instructions

1. Draw a curved line along the length of the wooden block. Find the middle of the shorter side and make a mark. Now draw a curve from this mark along the bottom of the length of wood. Add three indents into the bottom curve at the wide end to create wavy areas for your fingers.

2. Cut out the blank using your pocket knife. Do not worry about hollowing out the waves at this point, just carve the basic shape along the longer curves.

3. Use your hook knife to cut the waves into the wood, ensuring the cuts are smooth.

4. Remove wood shavings all around the front of the handle to make it thinner as it reaches the front. Also, smooth out any rough edges around the rest of the handle.

5. Let your handle rest on the wavy part so that you can see the top. Draw a 1 ½" line from the front of the handle. Cut onto the line, remove shavings as you go along, so that the blade can fit into the handle. Drill a small hole into each section of the tip, about ½" from the front.

6. Sand the handle and apply mineral oil to finish it off.

7. Assemble your pizza wheel by placing the blade into the handle and securing it with the screw. All you need now is a pizza!

Kuksa (Drinking Cup)

A kuksa is a drinking cup with a handle. This cup project is ideal if you want to scoop fresh spring water while on a camping trip. Balsa or basswood is a lightweight and soft choice for this cup, and won't add extra weight to your camping gear. A pocket knife forms the basic shape but you need a hook knife to hollow out the cup. It takes about 40 minutes to make and you need a piece of wood measuring roughly 6" x 4" x 4".

Instructions

1. Use a compass to draw a 4" circle at one end of the longer side. Draw a 1 ½" wide rectangle that connects to the circle and extends to the end of the block. Create a smooth curve where the rectangle joins the circle. This side is the top of the block. Cut along this

outline to create a blank. Shave away some of the rectangular handle edges to make it round.

2. Draw a circle with a 3 ⅓" diameter on the top of the block inside the previous circle. Turn the shape so that you can see the side. Draw a handle shape into the rectangular part but leave it open at the bottom. The handle should look like an inverted "L". You can curve the handle slightly too. Also, draw lines onto the cup section to depict roundings.

3. Use your pocket knife to shave away wood surrounding the handle so that you can hold it.

4. Use thumb push strokes to remove extra wood around the cup section and curve it a curved structure.

5. Turn the cup over so that you can see the top. Create a divot in the middle of the circle using the hook knife then shave away the inside of the cup. The interior circle marks the rim, so widen the hollow to there and then work on deepening the cup.

6. Use your pocket knife to round the edges of the rim.

7. Sand the cup, especially the rim and handle, then oil with a food-safe product.

Little Bird

A whittled bird is a beautiful addition to any windowsill or garden pot. This little bird helps in mastering rounding cuts but the basic shape gives you a lot of freedom. These birds require a coat of paint to make them identifiable. Give them to your kids or other children to paint if you do not want to paint them. Basswood or balsa is best for this project as it is soft and you may need to go against the grain at times so softer wood is better. Any size wood is fine, although a good start is 3" x 2" x 1". You need a pocket knife or flat steel blade for this project.

Instructions

1. Place your wood block so that the 3" x 2" side faces you. Draw a bird onto the wood. An easy way to do it is to draw a very loose "2" then add a beak to the front of the two and extend the bottom line for a tail section. If you are stuck, then get an outline image of a bird on the internet and transfer it to the wood.

2. Start whittling using paring cuts. Work from the beak over the top of the head and around to create the basic shape.

3. Next, whittle from underneath the beak, over the neck area and round the stomach to the bottom of the bird.

4. Whittle from the back of the head out and downward to create the tail feather. The bottom of the wood is not being whittled.

5. Using paring strokes, round out all sides of the bird to give it a more lifelike appearance.

6. Smooth the wood by sanding. You may want to drill two holes into the bottom of the bird to add plastic feet or thin dowels.

7. Paint the bird in any color your heart desires!

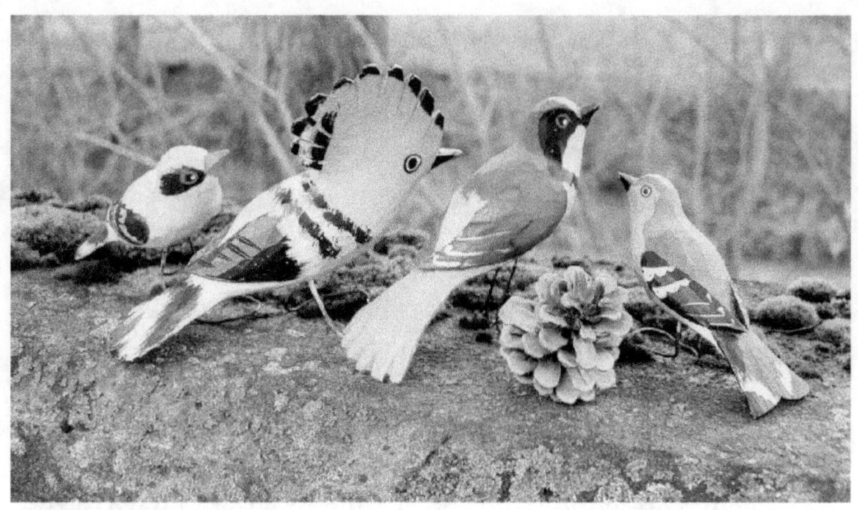

Mushroom

Whittling a mushroom allows you to practice your paring cuts, roundings, and thumb push strokes. A 1" thick branch or a basswood block works well for this project, as it is soft and easy to shape. Do not worry about precise measurements for this design, rather focus on your cutting technique and the feel of the wood. The length of the mushroom is about 2". A pocket knife will suffice, although some people prefer a raindrop razor edge for this project. The mushroom can be made in under 15 minutes, but take your time to master the techniques.

Instructions

1. Draw a cross on the top of the branch or cylinder, then use it to help draw a circle. On the sides of the block, draw a line about ¾" down from the top, then draw a triangular shape representing the top of the mushroom above each of the lines. Draw a stem onto the rest of the block. The stem should start small

under the top of the mushroom and gradually grow larger towards the bottom.

2. Using a rocking motion, create a deep cut line at the bottom edge of the mushroom's top.

3. Work from the cut line and shape the top of the mushroom using thumb push strokes. You want to get a round triangular shape.

4. Start shaping the stem by creating a notch at the cutting line. Use thumb push strokes or paring cuts to shave off wood from the cutting line to the base of the mushroom. You can deepen the cutting line as you remove more wood for the stem. The final stem, where it meets the top of the mushroom, should be about one-third the size of the mushroom's hood. Keep the stem thin at the top then widen it towards the base.

5. Use paring strokes to shape the bottom edge of the mushroom's hood. It should be round in shape. This section is fidgety, so work carefully.

6. Sand the mushroom and then paint it in any colors you like!

Dinosaur

Who doesn't love mythical creatures? This little dinosaur is a fantastic project and the perfect gift for a child. A pocket knife can work but this dinosaur has parts that require a sharp-pointed knife. A flat steel blade or raindrop razor edge makes whittling easier. Choose a softwood like balsa or basswood with straight grain for this project. Start with a block of wood measuring about 5" x 2" x 1". This dinosaur can take up to an hour to whittle.

Instructions

1. Turn the wood block so that a 5" x 1" side faces you. Measure about 1" down from the top and make a cut into the wood. This section will be the head. Measure another 1" down and draw a pencil line, with another line ⅓" down. These lines will hold the hands. Measure ⅓" from the bottom of the block and draw a line, which represents the feet. Then measure 1" up from this line and make a pencil marking in the middle of the block. This section will form the legs of the dinosaur. You may want to make some markings around the block to designate these areas.

2. Use your knife to and carve the head into an oblong shape. It should be thinner in the front and rounders along the top and back. Paring cuts work well to shape the head. Thin the wood out significantly as you reach your marked head line, so that the thinner part forms the neck. At the front of the block, use V-cuts and paring cuts to shape the head into a kidney bean-shape until the neck is about ⅔" thick from the back.

3. Draw a round eye on each side of the head and a line for the mouth on the front. Make a notch using a V-cut to create a groove for the mouth. Shape the eyes by using a pointed knife to cut around the eyes and whittle away excess wood, adding further definition to the head.

4. Cut about ½" into the top marking for the arms. Use paring strokes and thumb push cuts to remove wood

from the bottom of the head to this ½" marking but keep it at an angle so that the neck gently widens towards the arms. On the front of the dinosaur, draw two large ovals between the arm lines. Shape the wood around these oval shapes to create the arms. You can add some additional lines to the sides if you want to lengthen the arms into the body. Work carefully on this section as the workspace is tight.

5. At the bottom of the hands, cut ⅓" into the wood and shape all around the dinosaur to continue the shape from the top. Use paring cuts to extend the body and make it wider as you reach the marking for the dinosaur's legs. This section should be the widest part. It can be flatter in the back and rounded at the front.

6. Cut ½" into the line for the feet and take this line all around the wood. Gently whittle the back of the wood using V-cuts to create a slight indentation representing the hind legs and bottom of the dinosaur. You could add a small tail section at this point.

7. Turn to the front of the dinosaur. Using paring strokes, carefully whittle from the front leg marking (middle mark) to the front leg marking. Keep your movements round. Use V-cuts to segment the feet from the legs but keep the cuts round. Make a V-cut in between the feet to create individual feet. Whittle the feet shape to become rounder and more realistic. Finally, shape the inside part of each leg by making wide V-cuts from the front of each leg and into the middle of the piece.

8. Sand your dinosaur and apply mineral oil to the
   finished product. Alternatively, paint it to your liking.

Dog

This dog starts with a two-dimensional blank pattern
and transforms into a lifelike figurine. Find an outline of a
dog on the internet to use as our pattern. This dog is made
from soft basswood for easy whittling. A straight grain piece
measuring 2" x 2" x ¾" is perfect for this project. Use a
raindrop razor edge knife to get into all the tight spots. Be
careful when whittling the ears and tail, as they can come off
with a single misplaced cut. It takes about 25 minutes to
whittle this pup.

Instructions

1. Trace the dog pattern onto the wood. Add in any lines
   giving the detail, such as the hind leg moving into the
   hip. Use your knife to cut out the blank.

2. Use V-cuts to define the space between the legs and
   ears. Carve these out carefully. Also, add a V-cut for
   an open mouth.

3. Paring strokes help in forming the back to become
   rounder. Next, shape the rounding of the backside.

4. Work on the forelegs and then the hind legs to add
   definition. Make a small V-cut on each side of the leg
   and shave a round from this area into the chest,
   abdomen, or sides.

5. Shape the head by using paring strokes from the top
   of the head and move towards the snout, rounding the
   edges as you go along. Also shape the ears, making

them rounder at the back and pointed at the top. Carve a small V-cut into the inner ear for added detail.

6. Whittle the tail by starting at the base of the body and moving to the tip. Let it go from thicker to thinner at the tip.

7. Add small grooves into each paw to indicate the fold as the dog stands. Adding thin, vertical V-cuts to the front of each paw creates toes.

8. Add facial features by carving two eyes using V-cuts and a triangle for the nose.

9. Sand the final dog to remove any roughness. Paint the dog or add eyes and a nose using a marker.

Fish

Fish are a versatile whittling project. There are many different shapes and sizes to whittle. Try going for a bass fish or shark. If you are up for a challenge, then attempt a Chinese fighter fish or puffer fish where you can practice grooves. For this fish use 12" x 5" x 3" basswood, as it is soft enough to shave long segments from the base. You need to find a fish pattern on the internet to use as a template. A pocket knife works great for this project as there are no tight crevices. The size of the fish makes it a longer project but you should complete it within an hour.

Instructions

1. Transfer the fish pattern to one side of the basswood. It is advisable to also place the wood on its side as if the fish was swimming and then draw a top view of the fish onto this side. Think about whether your fish

is swimming in a straight line or whether the body is moving side to side through the water. Use this as a basis for the top perspective to make a straight fish or create curves.

2. Use straight rough cuts to take wood off the sides of the fish until you are left with the basic outline. It takes some time and numerous cuts, especially around the fins.

3. Working from the head towards the tail, start shaping the body of the fish using leverage cuts. It may be useful to cut in detail lines around each fin as a stopping guide or to notch from these segments in shaving the body design. The middle of the fish behind the gills should be the thickest part of the body. The head area is thinner. As you move from the middle to the tail, taper the width of the body so that it gradually thins out at the tail.

4. Start working on the fins and shaping them using paring or leveraging cuts. Make the fins a lot thinner than the body and taper the size as you reach the end of each fin. Some additional shavings to the body might be necessary as you work on the fins.

5. Make a definitive groove cut along the base of each fin, including the tail, to accentuate the design. Add several V-cut grooves to each fin for texture. They do not have to be parallel to each other; just make the cuts as your knife finds the wood.

6. Sand the body removing any leftover slivers.

7. Draw gills, eyes, and a mouth onto the fish. You can add any other details you wish. Accentuate these features by using V-cuts of different depths. At this stage, your fish is complete but don't let me stop you. Add some scales, extra curves or paint to your design.

Eagle Feather

The eagle feather is a fun whittling project. It is ideal if you want to practice V-cuts and making grooves. The finer details in this feather work best with balsa or basswood since it has less grain, which makes the grooves easier to whittle. Any size flat wood can work, for example, a pallet or thin plank lying around. A good size is 14" x 3" x ⅜". The feather takes at least 30 minutes to whittle but do not rush the grooves. Take your time and master this technique. The raindrop razor edge knife works best for this design.

Instructions

1. Draw a large feather on the wood. Remember to add a thin shaft through the middle of the feather. The shaft should start about 2" from the tip of the feather and extend about 1" after the end of the feather. Add a slight rounding to the tip of the feather so that it resembles an eagle's beak. Draw in the head section of the eagle by pencilling in a "v" from the shat to the outside of the feather. Draw the length of the beak into the head and add an eye. Draw three to five open notches into each side of the feather.

2. Start whittling by carving the outline. Shave off any extra wood using the thumb push cut or paring strokes, rounding the edges of the feather.

3. Make a V-cut next to each section of the sheath.
    Whittle the feather in broad strokes so that it is
    thinner than the sheath. Also, make a V-cut groove in
    the "v" formed between the head and shaft.

4. Remove the notches drawn into the wood by making a
    V-cut. Add a deep groove from each notch to the
    sheath. Add additional grooves, varying in depth, over
    the entire feather.

5. Using the tip of the raindrop razor edge, carve a beak
    line and eye socket into the top of the design.

6. Sand the design then paint it. Usually, the head is
    white, the beak and eye yellow with a touch of black,
    and the feather is tan or light brown.

Wood Spirit Idol

This spirit idol is a fun whittling project to do while you
are taking a break from hiking or sitting around the campfire
during your vacation. It is a great beginner project. Use a
thick twig or thin branch for this idol, about 1" in diameter
and 4" long. Just pick up a nice piece lying around the park
or forest - the size does not matter in this design. A simple
pocket knife does the trick for this project and you need a
marker too. It takes about 20 minutes to make the spirit idol.
This design is a creative one, so just go with the flow.

Instructions

1. Draw a nose in the middle of the length of wood. Add
    thick eyebrows and eyes. Draw a moustache under the
    nose and add an upwards facing half moon for the
    bottom lip. Also, draw a beard that attaches to the
    moustache.

2. Work from the top of the face and move down. Cut
    into the lines for the eyebrows using the tip of a
    pocket knife. Use a V-cut to define the top line. Leave
    the bark on the eyebrows. Cut out the eyes using a
    deeper chip-cutting method.

3. Shave off the face area between the nose, eyes, and
    moustache. Add some extra groves around the nose to
    produce features. Vary the depths of the slivers so that
    it creates cheekbone lines.

4. Remove the first layer of the bark over the eyebrows.
    Leaving the inner layer should give a darker color to
    the eyebrows. Peel all the bark off the nose.

5. Use a V-cut to remove the lip area between the
    moustache and beard.

6. Cut a groove into the lines for the moustache and
    beard. Remove the top bark layer of the beard so that
    some inner color remains. Do the same with the
    moustache.

7. Make a few V-cuts into the beard for extra detail and
    clean up any parts that still look a bit rough.

Yoda

Yoda, a recognizable and favorite character of many
people, can be made from wood too! This design uses a basic
Yoda outline with his hands in front of him. Yoda is cut from
a 3" x 1 ½" x ¾" balsa or basswood block, using a raindrop
razor edge knife or flat steel blade. The facial features and
ears are most important, so you want a precision blade for
this project. It takes about 40 minutes to whittle and some
more time to paint Yoda into his familiar colors.

Instructions

1. Find a Yoda image on the internet with his hands folded in front of him. Draw this image onto your wood.

2. Whittle the basic outline by making straight rough cuts around all sides of the wood. Focus on making V-cuts between the head and shoulders and use push cuts around the arms and body.

3. Round the square edges around the body and coat until it resembles the Yoda form.

4. Work on the head next. Shave it into an elliptical shape while leaving the ears in place. Then, use thumb push strokes to define the ears into their familiar shape. Thin the wood out from the head towards the tip of the ear. Add a slight V-cut into the front of the ear for definition. Flatten the top of the head slightly for a more realistic image.

5. Draw on the eyes, nose, and mouth. Make deep V-cuts for the eyes so that the nose stands out. Make shallower V-cuts for the forehead creases. Connect these cuts to each other for the almond-shaped eyes. Cut an inverted "U" shape underneath the nose for the mouth area. Then make a shallow groove within this area as lips.

6. Shape the neck area more as needed and add the "V" over the chest to resemble Yoda's coat.

7. Draw the folds of the coat and hands onto the body of Yoda. Make a cutting line around the hands and folding arms. Use V-cuts and paring strokes to widen

the cutting lines over the body, forming the shape as you go. Round out the arms.

8. Sand your Yoda and then paint it using the traditional colors.

Valentine's Heart

A gift for the love of your life, although your mom would like this heart too! This simple heart is made from any softwood. It uses basic techniques and is perfect for finishing up scrap segments of wood leftover from other projects. A square block of wood is necessary and it should be ¼" thick. Use a flat steel blade or your pocket knife. This design is so quick that you can finish it in 15 minutes with painting.

Instructions

1. Draw a heart in the middle of the wood but leave at least ⅓" of wood exposed around all sides. You can make the heart smaller too.

2. Use the tip of the knife to make a cutting line on the border of the heart. Make a groove using the cutting line as a guide.

3. Now, focus on the area surrounding the heart. Create texture by making vertical V-cuts over this entire area. Some grooves can be shallow and others deeper. The spacing is up to you too.

4. Using the paring stroke, create a beveled edge all around the block of wood.

5. Sand the edge briefly to remove any slivers.

6. Paint the heart in red and its outline with black or burgundy color. Add a dark wood stain to the etched area. Let it dry and give your heart away!

Hatching Easter Chick

Easter eggs are cool but one that lasts forever is better! This Easter egg has an added feature - it is hatching. Made from a 2" x 1 ½" x 1 ½" block of balsa or basswood, it is a great beginner project using several cutting techniques. Be careful when whittling the feet as they are fidgety and you might cut them off inadvertently if your knife is blunt. The shape and detail in this design make it a longer project: it takes about 45 minutes for the whittling section and then you have to paint it. A raindrop razor edge is the best knife for this egg since it has a lot of little details. A flat steel blade could work too.

Instructions

1. Draw a line that is ⅜" wide along the left and right-hand length of each rectangular side. On one of the rectangular sides (this will be the front) add ⅜" wide line along the shorter bottom side. This area will be for the feet.

2. Starting making straight rough cuts from this bottom line towards the top of the block in a rounding manner. The round shape on the other sides can be made from the very bottom of the wood to the top. Remember that the top of the egg is slightly smaller than the bottom, so keep that in mind while shaping the egg.

3. Shape the top of the egg using paring cuts as you have to cut across the grain. The top of the egg should be about ½" in height. Draw the cracked edge in using "v" shapes. Do not cut it yet; only do the basic shaping.

4. The bottom is wider and about ¾" high. Draw a cracked "v" edge along this line, but do not cut along it yet. We are only shaping the egg at the moment. Once you get to the front, make V-cuts around the feet and then use the chip technique to remove wood and round out the eggshell.

5. Define the edges of the cracked egg by making V-cuts all around. Widen these cuts with paring cuts to create a smoother chick body between the shell pieces.

6. Draw large elliptical eyes and an inverted triangle beak into the body. It can take up the entire front section as the rest of the body is hidden by the egg. Cut a groove around each eye and the beak. Next, give these features a bit of shape using paring cuts.

7. Shave away areas around the face and body so that the cracked shell extrudes beyond the hatched chick.

8. Finally, focus on decorating the shell. Use any designs you want. Add grooves, use the chip technique to cut triangles, or make some diamond shapes. You could even make two cut marks all around each shell part and use the V-cut method to hollow out this line.

9. Sand your product and then move onto the paint. The chick is yellow and the egg any colors you want. Pay attention to painting the eyes with white and creating

pupils using black or blue. Orange paint adorns the beak and feet. This chick plans on being around for ages!

Jack-O-Lanterns

Jack-O-Lanterns pop up everywhere during autumn and just in time for Halloween. Traditionally, they are carved from pumpkins. Many of the techniques used for these carvings are similar to whittling cuts. But, you can make your Jack-O-Lanterns last the entire year by making them from wood. Create them any size you want using balsa, basswood, or pine. Any scrap wood can do because you can change the pumpkin size according to your piece of wood. Make large ones for decorations, or tiny ones to add into a child's trick-or-treat container. Your wood should be ⅓" thick for small lanterns and 1" thick if you are making a lantern that is wider than 12". A pocket knife works well for this project but other knives make detail work easier.

Instructions

1. Draw a pumpkin on your wood slab - any shape is fine. Remember to ass a stem and use up as much of the wood as possible because it lessens the amount of wood to whittle.

2. Use your pocket knife to shave away the excess wood. Use a thumb push stroke to whittle around the stem.

3. Draw eyes, a nose, and a mouth with teeth onto the front. Use a raindrop razor edge or flat steel blade to cut these features into the wood. You can deepen the features by making more cuts. V-cuts work well for the teeth or to add details to the stem.

4. Finish the Jack-O-Lantern by sanding it till smooth. Add some paint and display your lantern. Jack-O-Lanterns are an easy sell at markets too, so you might want to make a few.

Snowman Ornament

Get into the festive spirit by whittling a snowman! This design has more details than some of the other projects, but it is suitable for beginners - simply follow the steps carefully. Use a 4" x 1.25" x 1.25" block of basswood. You want the softest wood possible due to the level of detail. The snowman provides practice of all the whittling techniques. A flat steel blade or raindrop razor edge is the best option for making a snowman. This design requires several measurements and drawings, so leave at least an hour for this snowman.

Instructions

1. Turn the square wood face towards you. Draw a 1" circle on this side, which will be the top of the snowman. In the top, right corner, write the number one and number each corner moving in a clockwise direction.

2. Draw a 1.25" circle on the bottom of the block of wood. We will get to it later.

3. Along the length of the block, measure from the bottom to mark out the brim of the snowman's hat. Measure 3 ⅜" at corner one; 3 ¼" at corner two and four, and; 3 ⅛" for corner three. Draw straight lines around the block to connect these marks on each corner.

4. Remove the wood from the 1" circle at the top up to the brim of the hat. Use V-cuts and push strokes to shape the round hat. Make it a bit rounder at the top, especially towards the front corner (one). You can keep the hat square or round the corners and slope the edges down for a floppy hat.

5. Now measure out the lower brim of the hat from the bottom of the snowman. Measure 3 ⅛" for corner one; 3" for corners two and four, and; 2 ⅞" for corner three.

6. Cut around the lower brim to the 1" diameter mark. Round the corners slightly that go towards the head.

7. Measure 2 ½" from the bottom and draw a line around the block. Draw a second line ¼" below this line. These lines represent the scarf.

8. Use V-cuts in a rounding manner to shape the head between the scarf and lower brim of the hat. Also, carve the scarf to become round and add small cuts into it for added texture.

9. Make V-cuts at the lower edge of the scarf to start creating the body of the snowman. Push these cuts to meet the 1" markings of the hat.

10. Let corner one face towards you. Draw on a face and body features like arms or a coat. Cut into each of these drawn lines to distinguish the features. Then, using V-cuts extend these features and use paring cuts to round out the body. Shave off areas between the arms and body for extra depths. Attach a small shaving for the nose.

11. Sand the entire snowman. Your ornament is ready for
    paint and then the tree!

Chapter 6:
Turning It Into a Business

Whittling is a productive and fun hobby that benefits your mind and spirit. Friends and family often admire whittled pieces too, so share the beauty of your art with them. You do not have to do whittling just as a hobby or give pieces away for free. You can also make money from it. Even if your main aim is just keeping yourself busy, the extra money can pay for your hobby. You can reinvest the cash into more wood and knives, which essentially makes your hobby cost-free!

Selling your whittling pieces is a chance for additional income while doing what you love. You could sell items to strangers, or even just to friends and family members. Some whittlers charge a lot, but you might feel more comfortable charging a small fee to cover the cost of the wood. That is fine too. It is much better to sell your items, rather than just adding to a growing collection that gathers dust. Share your creative genius! Anyway, who wouldn't like a little extra cash?

How Much Should I Charge?

Whittling projects sell for various amounts. It depends on the type of project, design, and selection of wood. Small projects that take about 20 minutes to complete, sell for about $20 in the right market. Projects requiring advanced skills have greater worth, starting from approximately $50, while larger projects can sell for much higher prices.

There are numerous ways to make money from whittling. For a start, think of creating a set of items, which you can sell together and bring in more money. You might whittle a cutlery set consisting of four each spoons, forks, and knives. Or, maybe your creative juices are flowing and you carve an entire chess set. Another popular option is holiday ornaments for Christmas, Easter, or Hanukkah. Alternatively, think of something that many people use, such as canes or walking sticks and whittle several of that item.

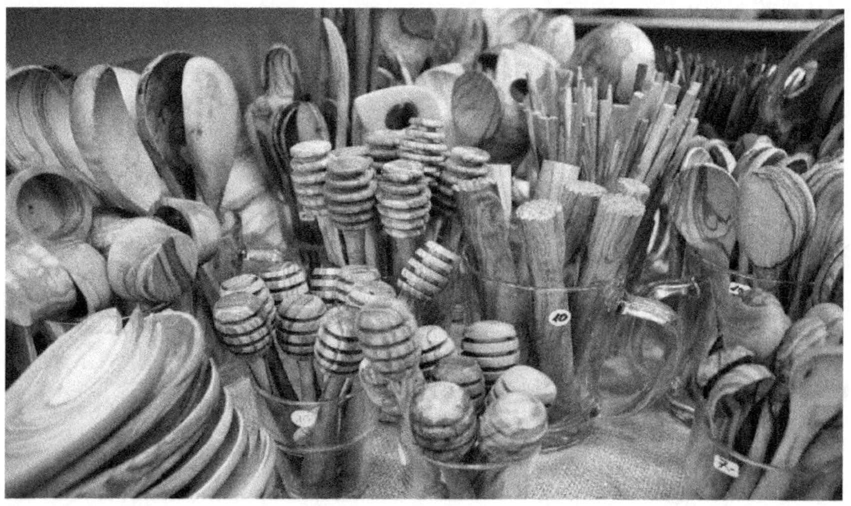

The amount you charge depends on the available market. You could advertise your whittling projects to family and friends. Another option is to find a local crafter's market, concert, or fair where you can display your products for sale. Remember to think outside the box at these events. Show several examples, even ones you do not want to sell and take orders for personalized items.

Increase the Value of your Artworks

In my opinion, money does grow on trees. Think about it - wood comes from trees; you need wood to whittle; selling whittled objects brings in money! But, there are ways to add more value to your artworks and increase the price you charge.

Ensure you create high-quality items. Using suitable wood and finishing a product well increases its value. Remove any rough areas of the wood by sanding it thoroughly using various grits of sandpaper. A smooth product is especially important when making wooden toys for children.

Give your product aesthetic qualities. Add some interesting details to your design by making grooves, holes, or other fine details. You can select a beautifully textured block of wood for a natural appeal and simply oil it once you are done. Otherwise, add color to your whittled item using paint. Just have fun with it and let your creative juices flow free.

A website and social media accounts add value to your business too. An online presence provides legitimacy and credibility. It shows you are serious about your business and lets you charge more because your work becomes popular. A website is optional since it can increase your costs but it does give another platform to sell your products or obtain orders. Social media pages, like Facebook or Instagram, provide you with a platform to advertise your work and share photos of your latest whittling projects. Encourage your friends and family to like your social media accounts and share this page with other people.

Promoting Your Work

There are several online marketplaces where you can sell your products. Ebay and Etsy are popular choices among craft enthusiasts. Facebook and Pinterest have store capabilities too, which is a great option if you have social media pages for your whittling business. Handmade Amazon is a reliable website where you can advertise your designs and it has a lot of visitors, so getting sales should be easy.

Display your whittling projects at various locations. Flea markets and art shows are an ideal place as visitors to these markets expect creative objects. They are more open to artistic talents and visit the market specifically to find something unique. There are also wood carving exhibitions and shows where woodcarvers come together to share their work and knowledge. These events are a great opportunity to meet other whittlers and pick up good deals on tools.

A big part of promotion is branding. Brand your business and create an identity for it. Start by choosing a name for your business, even if it is just for pocket money, and make a logo. Your logo might be a drawing of a pocket knife, a whittled item, or even just a tree - anything goes and you can be as creative as you want! Choose a single color, or several complementary colors, that identify with your business. Use this name, logo, and colors to link your products with your business.

Branding is a fun way to hone in on your skill set and style. For example, a person who likes stars might carve a small star into each whittled product, or your style might focus on woodland creatures. The world is your oyster so create any style you please. A specific style might not be present immediately. Give it some time and soon you will see repetitive design elements or a certain style emerging in your work.

Branding also helps other people to identify your artworks and remember how great you are at your craft. Some businessmen take it one step further by adding branding to their products. This branding may include a tag with a logo and contact number on it. Other people have stickers made with the logo and add it onto their artworks. It is always a good idea to add your number to your branding, as it gives people a way to contact you and could lead to more business.

How-To Guide for a Whittling Workshop

A workshop is a designated working area for handicrafts or DIY projects. You might already have a workshop or work area at your home - it might be a shed, garage, or crafts' room. Workshops usually contain tools. New hobbyists often spend a lot of money on tools and materials, which adds extra costs to your work. Only purchase the tools you need for basic whittling; you can always purchase more tools if you need them for a specific project. The same goes for the wood - do not purchase a ton of wood. Only buy what you need at that moment.

Whittling as a side job requires dedication and time. Commit to spending time on your hobby for a certain number of hours each week. For example, you could decide on whittling for one hour on workdays and two hours on Saturdays and Sundays, so you are whittling nine hours a week. If you whittle a new design each day, then you will have seven items ready for sale by the end of the week! The most important thing in making money while whittling is having products to sell, so always schedule a time for whittling and have some projects in mind ahead of time.

A business plan is a good idea for serious whittlers. Develop a business plan to guide your business decisions and include important information. Write down your costs, any tools or equipment you need to get, marketing ideas, and your basic products. Jot down where you will sell your products and who your target market will be. A formal business plan is important if you consider whittling your full-time job. If it is just an extra income, then a less formal business plan is suitable. Ultimately, it is a guiding document to give your business a particular direction.

Any business has incomes and expenses, so you want to track these amounts. A simple spreadsheet is a great tool to keep track of the numbers, although some people opt for free accounting software. For each project, make a list of the raw materials you use - these include the wood, paint or oil, and any packaging materials. Also, add shipping costs if you have to deliver the products or arrange a courier to the delivery address. The total of all these costs is the expenses you incurred during the project. Now determine how much you want to sell your product for. The selling price should be more than the costs. Remember to add extra for your time and creativity put into the project.

Whittling is an Asset

Whittling as a hobby is an asset. But what is an asset? In short, it is something that holds and adds value. Take your pocket knife as an example. It probably only cost you a few dollars but it is used in all your whittling projects. If your knife cost $20 and you sold five whittled products for $20 each, then you made $100. The pocket knife has increased to five times its original value, as you cannot whittle without it.

Reinvest the profits from your whittling projects back into the business. Use the money to purchase additional tools and new information. New tools increase the scope of what you can carve - you may decide to purchase a hook knife so that you can make hollow objects, or clamps to hold your wood in place. Information provides value through empowering you with knowledge. Take a whittling class, purchase another book, or read up on new techniques.

As the money trickles in, your excitement will grow. Even if it is just a little bit of money, you know that these funds can purchase new tools and materials. Be sure to expand your knowledge constantly, learn new techniques, find out about specific wood, and listen to what customers want. Soon you will have a thriving side business and lucrative income while having fun practicing your hobby!

Conclusion

The numerous benefits of whittling make it a must-try for all people. It is beneficial for the mind, body, and spirit because it uses mental and physical capacity. Whittling equalizes your breathing, which lowers stress levels and blood pressure. You can think more clearly and forget about your daily strife. Whittling also improves your hand-eye coordination and fine motor skills, allowing your hands to become stronger. As a creative outlet, whittling encourages artistic thinking and enhances mental capacity.

The resources required for whittling are few, which make it an accessible hobby. With a pocket knife and some wood, you are soon on your way. Of course, the flat steel blade, raindrop razor edge, and hook knife are valuable additions to your whittling knife collection and increase the scope of your designs. Invest in proper knife sharpening tools to keep your blades in good condition.

An important part of whittling is your hands. Your hands play a part in every aspect of the craft, from holding the wood to moving the knife for cuts. Stretch your hands regularly to improve your range of motion and strength. Protect your hands by wearing suitable whittling gloves or finger guards. Rather spend a few moments getting used to the extra padding, than having to sit out for weeks because you cut yourself. Yet, be prepared for small nicks or cuts by having a first aid case close by your workstation. Regularly check your gloves for wear and buy new ones if yours are too old.

The wood you use can make or break a project. Softwoods like balsa, basswood, butternut and pine remain firm favorites for beginner projects. Although, I am not going to stop you if you decide to attempt a hardwood. Just remember to always cut with the grain and use wood that has dried properly. Always use a wood section that is large enough for your intended purpose but not that big that you are going to waste time cutting off big pieces. Purchase wood cut-to-size at a craft store or visit your local lumberyard if you need wood for larger projects.

So many stories come from whittling activities. Besides having fun when looking for pieces of wood while hiking, whittling is a hobby you can share with your friends and family. Empowering someone else with knowledge increases the endorphins in your body and leaves you feeling positive. Just think of the stories you can share with your friends, children, or grandchildren about a specific whittled heirloom. Whittling is a craft that continues through generations.

Wood carving has been around for centuries. From the beginning of time, humans understood the beauty and power of trees. Furniture and homes were and still are, made from wood. Early religious leaders used wood to share stories of their faith and artists whittled many sculptures of historical figures. Intricate carvings adorn places of worship and modern furniture values the natural hues from wood. Whittling, as a wood carving technique, has always been a part of this world. Wood carvings tell the story of days gone past and days to come. Are you ready to whittle your story?

Thank you for choosing my book and sharing my experiences with me! I trust that the information in this book empowers you to start a new hobby. Hopefully, you have already tried some of the projects as you worked through the chapters. If not, I encourage you to pick up a knife and start whittling. I am sure you will enjoy it as much as I do! If you found this book helpful and positive, then please share your feedback by leaving a review.

May your whittling journey be filled with creativity, smiles, and interesting tales!

References

Allpastimes. (n.d.). *Wood carving a hobby for yourself.*
https://www.allpastimes.com/wood-carving

Anapur, E. (2017). *The history of wood carving in art.*
Widewalls.
https://www.widewalls.ch/magazine/wood-carving-
wooden-sculpture-art

"BeaverCraft sloyd knife C4s 3.14." (n.d.).
https://www.amazon.com/dp/B07NWWTVW8/?tag=
best-whittling-knife-20

Bellarmine University. (2005). *Basswood.*
https://www.bellarmine.edu/faculty/drobinson/Bass
wood.asp#:~:text=Basswood&text=Interesting%20In
formation%20About%20Plant%3A,North%20Americ
a%3B%20its%20native%20habitat

Brian. (n.d.). *Comparison of different safety gloves for
whittling.* Carving is fun.
https://carvingisfun.com/whittling-gloves/

Brightwater. (2019). *5 Big benefits of creative expression.*
https://brightwatergroup.com/news-articles/5-big-
benefits-of-creative-expression/

Carving is fun. (n.d.). *10 Reasons why you should start
whittling.* https://carvingisfun.com/why-you-should-
start-
whittling/#It%E2%80%99s_a_Fun_and_Relaxing_P
astime

David. (2016). *Make money selling wood carvings*. Artistic Wood Products. https://artisticwoodproducts.com/tips-and-tricks/make-money-selling-wood-carvings/

Duncan, B. (2017). *The basics of sharpening*. Woodcarving Illustrated. http://woodcarvingillustrated.com/blog/2017/09/08/basics-sharpening/#:~:text=The%20more%20force%20required%20to,that%20is%20not%20shaped%20properly.

Jefferson, S. (n.d.(a)). *Whittling basics - best tool for wood carving, cuts & more*. Woodcarving 4u. https://woodcarving4u.com/wood-carving-basics/#:~:text=V%2DCut,an%20angle%20to%20the%20surface.

Jefferson, S. (n.d.(b)). *Types of wood for carving - hardwood vs. softwood*. Woodcarving4u. https://woodcarving4u.com/types-of-wood-for-carving/

Jefferson, S. (n.d.(c)). *50+ Whittling projects ideas - full tutorials*. Woodcarving4u. https://woodcarving4u.com/50-whittling-projects-ideas/

Holmes, J. (n.d.). *Whittling for beginners: A guide to the basics*. Cool of the Wild. https://coolofthewild.com/whittling-how-to-whittle/

Iowa State University. (n.d.). *American basswood.*
https://naturalresources.extension.iastate.edu/forestr
y/iowa_trees/trees/basswood.html

Linker, D. (2020). *Carve a bear - woodcarving how to
tutorial.* YouTube.
https://www.youtube.com/watch?v=wxh1ezJEHzQ

Make from wood. (n.d.). *Whittling vs. woodcarving: which
hobby is best for you?*
https://www.makefromwood.com/the-differences-
between-whittling-and-wood-carving/

Merritt, C. (2019). *Assets vs. liabilities & revenues vs.
expenses.* Chron.
https://smallbusiness.chron.com/assets-vs-liabilities-
revenue-vs-expenses-52855.html

Nash, C. (2009). *What you need to know about carving
gloves.* Woodworkers Institute.
https://www.woodworkersinstitute.com/wood-
carving/techniques/ancillary-equipment/what-you-
need-to-know-about-carving-gloves/

Reitmeyer, R. (2002). *Understanding wood grain.* Whittlin'
Basics.
https://www.jrcarvers.com/index_htm_files/Handou
t_Understanding_Wood_Grain.pdf

Sharpen-Up. (n.d.). *How to whittle: A beginner's guide to
this wonderful craft.* https://www.sharpen-
up.com/how-to-whittle-beginners-
guide/#What_is_the_Best_Wood_for_Whittling

Stahl, A. (2018). *Here's how creativity actually improves
your health.* Forbes.

https://www.forbes.com/sites/ashleystahl/2018/07/
25/heres-how-creativity-actually-improves-your-
health/#668e065913a6

The Wood Database. (n.d.). *Black cherry*.
https://www.wood-database.com/black-
cherry/#:~:text=Common%20Uses%3A%20Cabinetr
y%2C%20fine%20furniture,Yellow%20Poplar%20(Lir
iodendron%20tulipifera).

Thomas, E. (n.d.). *Uses for cedar lumber*. SFGate.
https://homeguides.sfgate.com/uses-cedar-lumber-
99446.html#:~:text=One%20popular%20use%20for
%20cedar,also%20have%20insect%2Drepellant%20q
ualities.

TownCutler. (n.d.). *Care and maintenance*.
https://towncutler.com/pages/care-and-maintenance

Vermont Woods Studios. (n.d.). *Walnut wood*.
https://vermontwoodsstudios.com/content/walnut-
wood#:~:text=Black%20walnut%20wood%20is%20d
ark,wood%20develops%20a%20lustrous%20patina.

Vladimir. (2018). *3 Benefits of wood carving for body, mind
and spirit*. Home Wood Spirit.
https://homewoodspirit.com/wood-carving/3-
benefits-of-wood-carving-for-body-mind-spirit/

Vozza, S. (2020). *10 Tips to turn your hobby into a business*.
Legal Zoom. https://www.legalzoom.com/articles/10-
tips-to-turn-your-hobby-into-a-business

WebMD. (2020). *Slideshow: 10 ways to exercise hands and
fingers*.

https://www.webmd.com/osteoarthritis/ss/slideshow-hand-finger-exercises

Wikipedia. (2020). *Hardwood.*
https://en.wikipedia.org/wiki/Hardwood

Wikipedia. (2020). *Juglans cinerea.*
https://en.wikipedia.org/wiki/Juglans_cinerea

Wikipedia. (2020). *Ochroma.*
https://en.wikipedia.org/wiki/Ochroma#:~:text=It%20is%20evergreen%20or%20dry,is%20the%20softest%20commercial%20hardwood.&text=The%20name%20balsa%20comes%20from%20the%20Spanish%20word%20for%20%22raft%22.

Wikipedia. (2020). *Pine.* https://en.wikipedia.org/wiki/Pine

Wikipedia. (2020). *Softwood.*
https://en.wikipedia.org/wiki/Softwood

Wikipedia. (2020). *Whittling.*
https://en.wikipedia.org/wiki/Whittling

Woodcarver. (2018). *Best hook knives for easy spoon carving.* Best Wood Carving Tools.
https://www.bestwoodcarvingtools.com/best-hook-knives-for-easy-spoon-carving/

Woodcarver. (n.d.). *Best pocket knife for whittling.* Best Wood Carving Tools.
https://www.bestwoodcarvingtools.com/best-pocket-knife-for-whittling/

Woodcarver. (2016). *Fury Nobility Raindrop razor edge blade folding knife with rose pakka handle.* Best

Wood Carving Tools.
https://www.bestwoodcarvingtools.com/245-2/

Woodcarver. (2019). *How to make woodworking projects profitable*. Best Wood Carving Tools. https://www.bestwoodcarvingtools.com/how-to-make-woodworking-projects-profitable/

Wood Magazine. (n.d.). *Aspen*. https://www.woodmagazine.com/materials-guide/lumber/wood-species-1/aspen

Images in order of appearance:

https://burst.shopify.com/photos/pocket-knife-sharpens-stick?q=whittling

https://unsplash.com/photos/H7EFDGf84to

https://pixabay.com/photos/wood-knife-woodcarving-hobby-2726308/

https://www.pexels.com/photo/grayscale-photo-of-person-carving-block-1297938/

https://www.pexels.com/photo/green-leaf-plant-on-brown-wooden-stump-129743/

https://burst.shopify.com/photos/marking-wood-to-cut?q=spiral+pencil

https://pixabay.com/photos/wooden-table-ladle-wood-chopping-2562416/

https://cdn.pixabay.com/photo/2018/01/21/14/24/wooden-3096686_960_720.jpg

https://pixabay.com/photos/snowman-snow-winter-white-wintry-1872164/

https://pixabay.com/photos/workshop-handmade-honey-spoon-4845949/

Intermediate Guide to Whittling

15 Secrets Woodcarvers Should Know to Get Better

Ryan Feldman

Introduction

I grabbed the mallet from its spot on the wall and marched back outside. After securing the wood to the table, I carefully held the chisel in one hand and swung the mallet. It connected to the back of the chisel with a dull thud and I marveled at how easily the chip came away from the piece. Swing for swing, I carved out a new design with a newfound confidence in my skills. I was proud of myself: No longer did I just whittle; a whole new world of possibilities opened in front of my eyes.

***

Whittling has always been my first love and saving grace. As far back as I can remember, I walked through the forests of the Pacific Northwest searching for sticks to create a masterpiece with nothing more than a simple pocket knife. I loved finding a new piece of wood and imagining the possibilities. For a while, I lost my way getting caught up in drugs and petty crimes until I found my way back to my home and wood. Truly, woodcarving saved my life and got me back onto the straight and narrow.

Wood remains ever-present in my life today, both as a career and a hobby. I consider myself to be a lumberjack and forged a career in carpentry where I build homes. On the side, I practice my hobby, woodcarving, and have started earning a sizable income from doing what I love. Now, I want to share my passion and knowledge with you!

So you already know the basics of whittling and now your fingers are itching to try more techniques. Yet, you may wonder what the difference is between whittling and woodcarving. Whittling is a specific technique within wood carving, which mainly uses basic knives and handheld pieces of wood. It is a basic technique, so I am going to empower you with everything you need to know to take your hobby to the next level.

"Carving is a source of joy to the artist…To attack the raw material, gradually to extract a shape out of it following one's own desire, or, sometimes, the inspiration of the material itself: this gives the sculptor great joy." - Aristide Maillol.

The quote above shows the joy that wood carving can bring to a person while giving insight into the process. The wood is a blank canvas that can become the masterpiece of your imagination. Are you ready to bring out your artistic side and express yourself through learning new techniques? Yes? Great! I am with you every step of the way.

In this book, I am going to take your skills one step further by introducing new wood carving techniques. Many whittlers get bored with the basic designs and start experimenting with other cuts and tools. Intricate designs and larger pieces become an aspirational goal, however, a lack of knowledge prevents you from creating matching artwork. The techniques I show throughout the book will expand your repertoire while using many of the tools you already have in your workshop. These techniques are an extension of whittling and do not require specialized tools, although I will present some options for expanding your collection.

There are 15 secrets to wood carving that I share with you throughout this book. These secrets are important elements of wood carving and many provide motivation to improve your skills. These secrets address all types of things including new techniques, the best tools for a specific job, and how to use wood and make proper cuts. Additional secrets consider sharpening stones, wood finishes, and practical wood carving tips. So, without further ado, here is the first secret you should know:

Secret 1: *Woodcarving isn't a craft that relies only on skill and technique. It's incredibly important for a carver to have patience. Rushing and getting frustrated because things are not going the way they should will truly get you nowhere. You need to make mistakes, you have to damage and break many pieces of wood until you become fully proficient.*

A few hours of wood carving each week can change your life and has so many benefits. Wood carving is a calming activity, which reduces stress, improves your breathing, and lowers your blood pressure. The more you focus on the rhythmic cuts, the more your mind settles and your body soon releases dopamine, a feel-good hormone. Working with wood creates a connection between you and nature, which is food for the soul. It is an activity away from technological influence where you can set your mind free and let creativity blossom. The feeling of pride upon finishing a piece is incomparable to anything else; it is a rush of energy!

Even if you do get frustrated when the wood breaks, it is part of the learning process and teaches patience. Take a quick break when you get stuck and get your mind back in the game. Sometimes, a few minutes away from your project gives clarity of mind and you realize where you are making mistakes. This is a great time to sharpen your tools or tidy your workspace. A break also gives your hands a rest from hard work because wood carving is harsh on your hands and sometimes you just need to release that tension.

Secret Two: *Whittling and general wood carving can tire your hands and wrists. Instead of suffering, seek methods that strengthen your grip and wrists. Squeeze a pressure ball while watching television, do hand exercises for improved range of motion, or strengthen your wrists with yoga exercises.*

Stronger hands make wood carving much easier but your hands also strengthen as you practice more. It helps in controlling the knife and other tools, which makes precision cutting easier resulting in a product with a high-quality finish. There are other ways to improve the end product, such as choosing the correct type of wood and a suitable finish.

I have added numerous projects for you to try in this book, which help in improving your new skills. So let's get started with the first new techniques and some practice designs. I cannot wait to teach you more about wood carving!

Chapter 1:
Incised and Chip Carving Techniques

Whittling is the most basic wood carving technique that many of us learn from simply picking up a stick and hacking away at it with a knife. There is something magical about seeing the wood shavings flying all over the place. Once you have whittling under your belt, you can move onto new techniques and expand your skillset.

Some techniques necessitate a practiced hand for precise carving while using a range of tools. These techniques are suitable for individuals who have mastered intermediate techniques. Yet, you have to sharpen your skills (and knives) and grow your tool collection before learning advanced techniques. The next two chapters present these intermediate techniques for skill-building and act as a middle man between whittling and professional, complex wood carving.

Secret 3: Incised carving, chip carving, intaglio, and relief carving are separate wood carving techniques. Yet, the tools used in all four techniques are quite similar. Additionally, their basics have a heavy dependence on whittling cuts and techniques. When whittling is the first wood carving technique a person masters, they often attempt other carving projects without any trouble at all.

Incised Carving

Incised carving, sometimes called line carving, focuses on carving an outline. This technique reveals a two-dimensional image. A design or pattern is drawn onto a flat wood surface and then the outline is carved using specific tools. When I think about incised carving, it conjures images of school desks filled with graffiti. There was always something carved into the desk using a compass; a permanent memory for generations to come. Another familiar incised artwork is made by couples: a heart containing initials carved into the side of a tree. So, incised carving might be a technique that you have some knowledge of already. In its most simple form, it is a line.

Think back to your whittling techniques for a moment. A popular technique is the v-cut, which removes thin slivers of wood from your piece. Incised carving is similar to this method as it focuses on creating grooves, trenches, and lines. However, incised lines are thinner than v-cuts and are usually used on flat surfaces. You might have used a similar technique when adding details to your three-dimensional pieces, such as defining facial features.

Essential Tools

Although a simple pocket knife can work, specialized tools assist you in creating intricate incised designs. Gouges with a "v" or "u" shape and a veiner make incised carving a lot faster. The v-gouge produces an angled cut similar in shape to the results from a whittling v-cut. In contrast, the veiner and u-gouge generate a trench. Each design has its requirements regarding the best tool for the job, so read the instructions carefully or think about the design you want before starting. A veiner tends to produce a thinner line than gouges, so you might need a combination of tools for your design.

Practical Tips

Two tool grips are useful for incised carving: low grip and high grip. A low grip requires you to hold the tool at a small angle to the wood. The best way to do this is to hold the handle in the same way as you would a bicycle's handle. This grip is ideal for making long strokes using a push cut. With the high grip, hold the handle as if it was a pen so that there is a larger angle between the tool and wood. A high grip is necessary when working in tight areas and for creating curves or circles.

Decide on the depth of your carving before you start so that you know what you are working towards. Sometimes, shallow incisions will suffice but other designs require deeper cuts. A combination of depths is a sensible option too but determine the depth of each line so that there is consistency. There is nothing as bad as working hard and then realizing your piece is ruined by different line depths. Measure the depth of each line using a gauge; for example, mark the desired depth of each line on a toothpick. Insert the toothpick into the incision to see if you need to remove additional wood. Remember, it is best to go over the same line several times when removing wood, rather than making deep gouges that ruin the piece.

Project: Grab the Bull by the Horns

A bull design is a fantastic starting point when you want to practice the incised technique. The back and legs have longer strokes while the head, shoulders, and other areas have curves, so you can practice both grips in one piece. For this design, use a 10" x 6" x ½" piece of softwood, such as balsa or basswood. Do an internet search to find a picture of a bull and print it out to fit the piece of wood. You only want an outline, so select an image (called a pattern) that has long and curved lines but not too much detail. Let's get started:

1. Transfer the bull image to your piece of wood by drawing over the printout with a ballpoint pen. A light, indented design should be visible on the wood once you remove the paper. You might want to go over these lines with a pencil to see more clearly. Alternatively, use carbon paper while tracing the design. Just keep in mind that pencil and carbon marks may change the color of the wood, so you have to remove that with light sanding later on.

2. Using your tool of choice, start from the bull's shoulders and make a long stroke for the back. A low grip helps in maintaining a consistent depth. Make any additional long cuts wherever it is suitable for your design.

3. Change to a high grip and start working on incising the outline of the head, hooves, and other elements. Try to incise an eye using a rounding action.

4. Check the depth of your cuts continuously during the process. Go over any lines that require extra depth until the entire piece is complete.

Use only one tool the first time you make this design so that you get to know its grips and cuts. Once you are done with this project, repeat the process with a new tool but using the same image. You can do this as many times as you want and even try a combination of tools. It creates a great visual comparison for referencing and learning the difference between the tools.

Think about your finished product before you start incise carving. Usually, either the incised line or the background is accentuated in a contrasting color. If you want the background to be darker and the lines lighter, then you have to stain or varnish the wood and let it dry before you start carving. Alternatively, paint the incised lines once you are done carving.

Chip Carving

Chip carving is a decorative wood carving technique that has been around for centuries. Many gothic artworks, churches, doors, and trays feature intricately carved wood using chip carving. Usually, flat surfaces work best for this technique, although it is used to produce features such as eyes on rounded surfaces.

In its most basic form, chip carving requires several cuts from different angles and directions to remove a wood chip. Removing many wood chips reveals beautiful, ornamental designs. Cuts are made at an angle, which creates a bevel. The word "bevel" means angle or slant, indicating various depths within the design.

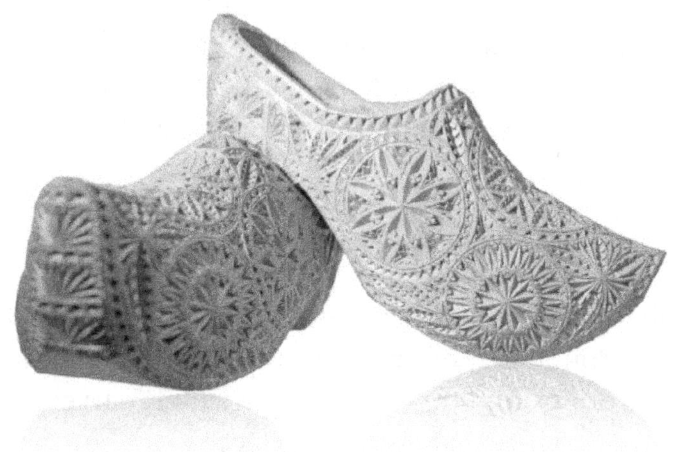

Chip carving is classified into two types that have distinct characteristics. The first type is fine triangle chip carving, which is exactly as the name says: removing triangular chips by following a pattern of lines. Fine triangle works well for intricate designs, such as flowers with a lot of detail, and to create consistent, repetitive designs. The second type is free-form chip carving. This method does not follow a specific pattern; rather, you make cutlines as you see fit from a suitable direction. Free-form works best in creating imaginative pieces, although most projects require a combination of these techniques.

Essential Tools

Various knives work best for chip carving. These knives include chip carving knives, stab knives, and detail knives. Your traditional pocket knife, flat blade, or raindrop razor edge work well, although you may want to invest in the additional tools as it makes chipping easier.

At some time, you are going to find that your knife cannot carve the chip you desire, usually because the wood is too hard. This is an indication that you should use a chisel and mallet for chip carving. A mallet is essential when wood becomes tough because you can remove chips more easily, while the chisel glides more easily through the wood. Use the chisel in a similar way as a knife but tap it lightly with the mallet so that it cuts into the wood.

Hand Positions

Chip carving requires specific hand positions during the carving process so that your design can come to life. These positions dictate your grip on the handle and the pivoting point, as removing chips necessitates a pivoting action.

- *Basic*: Hold the knife in a clenched hand with the top of the knife (where the blade meets the handle) resting on your index finger. Gently guide the tip of the blade into the wood at a 30 - 45 degree angle and use the handle as the pivot.

- *Straight wall*: The straight-wall position aims to create a cut that is almost perpendicular to the surface of the wood. Drive the blade into the wood using an 85 - 90 degree angle and focus on creating a deep cut. Usually, straight wall cuts are made along two sides of a triangle.

- *Curved edge*: Curves frequently appear in chip carving, especially when cutting flower petals or spiral designs. The key to the curved edge is changing the angle of your hand. Start at the tip of the pattern with the blade at a 45-degree angle. Decrease the angle to 30 degrees as you reach the center of the cut, then increase the angle after the middle so that it is back to 45 degrees by the time you reach the end. Think of this method in the same way as scooping food from a bowl.

- *Three or Four-sided*: Start by holding the knife in the basic position but use a 45-degree angle. Push the knife into one part of the shape at a time and press it towards the center of the shape.

- *Sloped floor to straight-wall*: This position requires a shallow cut that meets a straight wall (perpendicular) on one side. Use a knife with a flatter blade and hold it as flat as possible to the wood, almost horizontally, while pushing forward.

Practical Tips

Chip carving is not as challenging as it might seem and you have probably used some of these positions already. However, you can improve your skills by keeping a few things in mind while chip carving. Your hand position will make or break your cut so practice the method ahead of time. Do not rest your hand on the wood or table, as it changes the cutting angle. It is okay to rest your thumb on the table or wood since it creates a pivot point from which to work. Keep your wrist straight at all times to avoid changing your angle without your knowledge. Rather, move your knife from your elbow for consistent angles and smoother lines.

Chip carving is tiring on the hands. Many beginner carvers hold their knives too tight when chip carving because they think it gives better control. It is not the case and can cause you to cut too deeply, which ruins the piece. Your hands will hurt too, so keep a firm grip on the handle and stop if your hands start cramping. An ergonomic handle is advisable if you are going to hold a knife for a long time.

Many designs have repetitive patterns that require the same cuts to be made numerous times. It is best to cut the first side on all the shapes, then cut the second side, and then the first side. This method ensures uniformity among the design and makes it look more professional. Generally, chip carving requires one cut from each side to create the design. Cutting from the same side of a shape multiple times is not recommended as the angle and force may change the chip size, which creates an inconsistent result.

Ragged surfaces after chipping indicate one of two things. The wood may be too hard making it difficult for you to cut through in a swift motion. Using a mallet, apply a light force to the back of a chisel (not a knife), which makes it glide more easily and requires less strength from you. However, the more likely cause is a dull blade, so sharpen your tools properly and try again.

Project: Practice makes Perfect

A multitude of patterns and projects are available for chip carving. Truly, it is a wood carving technique that unleashes creativity because you can carve anything your heart desires. Before you start on intricate projects, you have to master the basic positions and cuts. Jumping into a specific pattern immediately might lead to disappointment if your cutting doesn't quite go to plan. So, start by practicing on a smooth, blank piece of wood. Clean a slab of butternut wood, about 12" x 10" x ½", to create a sampler board for practicing and grab your tools.

1. Draw parallel lines ½" apart across the length of the wood. Do the same along the width so that you are left with a grid.

2. Draw triangles in each block in the first row with the two rows below that forming larger triangles. Use the basic position to carve out one triangle in each block. Practice consistent cutting using the same angle for at least five blocks before changing the angle.

3. In the next available line use the four-sided position to cut a row of squares.

4. Draw half circles across the next row. Make a straight wall cut along the diameter of each circle. Next, carve out the half-circle using the curved edge position.

5. Over the next two rows, you can practice the sloped floor to straight-wall. Make a straight wall cut at the top of each square and then use the length of the two rows to create the sloped floor.

6. Use the remaining section of the wood for free-form chip carving. Draw ovals, curved lines, or other shapes and carve each one by changing the cutting angle and direction.

Softwoods are the best option for chip carving because they contain less grain and cut away easily. Butternut or balsa is soft enough to chip with little effort. However, you can chip carve harder woods such as mahogany or white oak. Dense woods are difficult to use in chip carving, so you require a mallet and chisel for proper use.

Secret 4: *Certain carving techniques perform better when combined with specific types of wood. Every* *woodcarver requires awareness of these winning carving combinations.*

Chapter 2:
Intaglio and Relief Carving

By now, you probably realize that you have been using some of these techniques already. Whittling is such a versatile hobby that learning new techniques comes to a person with little effort. The next two techniques are intaglio and relief carving. These techniques differentiate clearly between the foreground (or design) and the background (the wood surface. The main difference between the two carving techniques is these two levels. With intaglio, you are carving the design into the wood but with relief carving, you remove the background to reveal the design. Both techniques use elements of incised and chip carving, so mastering them is possible.

Intaglio Carving

Intaglio is a carving technique where the carver cuts a design into the wood and hollows out areas to create an image. It is similar to engraving, incised carving, and chip carving but the main difference lies in the larger areas of wood being removed, rather than just a line or chip. In fact, chip carving is a type of intaglio carving. The main design extends into the wood while the surface of the wood remains the background and at a higher level than the design. Some people call this reverse carving or negative relief carving, however, this book uses the traditional term, intaglio.

Intaglio carving is a popular technique for paneled items, like jewelry boxes, doors, and tabletops. Another use for intaglio is seen in furniture and moldings, where cutting into the work creates curves and crevices, like those often seen at the foot of a chair. Intaglio is the perfect technique if your finished piece will be used frequently because it will not chip away at the design, even if the raised surface experiences some damage. Patterned rolling pins, wax sealing stamps, and cookie presses all utilize the intaglio technique in the final product.

Essential Tools

Intaglio carving does not require specialized tools, although you may want to invest in additional gouges. Traditional whittling knives have flatter blades, except for hook knives that create curvature. Whittling knives can be used for intaglio but the artwork then requires a lot more cuts and producing consistent curvature becomes a challenge. It is much better to purchase gouges, which are used for other techniques too. Both u-shape and v-shape gouges are a valuable addition to your wood carving equipment.

Intaglio Carving Fundamentals

Seven cuts are fundamental for intaglio carving. Practice each cut before you start working on a project so that you understand the technique and create precise carvings. None of these methods are difficult but they do require some practice. It is also a good idea to make a practice board for yourself that shows each fundamental cut clearly for future reference. Hold your tool in a similar position as the basic cut for chip carving and keep the blade at a 30- to 45-degree angle to the wood.

Single Pass Trough

Measure the width of the gouge then draw two lines on a segment of wood, which are narrower than the gouge. Start at one end and place the gouge's edge between the two lines. Using a consistent force, push the gouge along the wood to create a trough-type shape. A u-shaped gouge creates a circular trough while the v-gouge produces a v-cut.

Double Pass Center Ridge

A ridge is a raised area between two troughs. Create a ridge by drawing three parallel lines instead of two. Next, create a single pass trough between the first two lines, then make a single pass trough between the next two lines. The line in the middle should remain raised to form the ridge. Creating this ridge requires a precise hand for maximum straightness and effect.

Square-Sided Trough

Sometimes, you want a trough with clear cut sides and a more angular design. A square-sided trough has well-defined sides that meet in a deeper v-cut. For this technique, you require a v-gouge that is narrower than the trough you are carving. Start by drawing parallel lines wider than the gouge. The square-sided trough requires multiple passes, so carve the left side, then the right, and finally the middle. Place the "v" of the gouge on the left line and angle the blade so that it is square along the line. Use a smooth stroke to carve the left edge of the trough. Repeat the process to create the right edge of the trough. Next, carve the middle of the trough by placing the v-gouge upright, producing a definite corner within the trough.

Single Pass Ellipse

Draw an ellipse with the widest part being smaller than the gouge. Place the blade at the edge of the ellipse and cut lightly into the wood. Increase the pressure slightly while following the two lines on the sides of the gouge so that the cut widens. Lighten the pressure when you pass the middle so that you can carve the ellipse smaller towards its rounded edge. Reaching the end of the ellipse may create a long chip that obscures the drawn lines, so you might want to break off the chip and then continue carving for a precise rounding.

Multiple Pass Ellipse

This technique is necessary when the ellipse is wider than the gouge. Start by making a trough-type cut along the middle of the ellipse. Next, place the blade on the left-side line and follow the line to make the next pass. Keep a consistent angle so that the cut lines up with the previous one. Repeat this process on the other side to create a complete ellipse. Depending on the size of the ellipse, you may require more passes.

Cup

A cup shape is a great option when you want to create only part of an ellipse. Think of it as half of an ellipse, or a half-circle. Draw an ellipse half and close off the opening with a straight line. Make the cut with a gouge using the single-pass ellipse technique but stop at the straight edge. Use a straight blade knife and cut along the straight line to stop the cut, then remove the chip.

Globe Cut

Although ellipses are great, there are times when you want a perfect circle or globe shape, like when you create eyes in a carving. Make a circle on your wood by placing the edge of the gouge perpendicular to the surface and rotate it around its axis - you should be left with a perfect circle. Do not press too hard, as you just want the basic shape. Next, angle your blade for the depth you want and pass it around the circle several times until a round wood chip comes loose from the center. Scoop out this piece, then smooth out the globe by making additional passes. A round incision should have shadows on the inside due to the depth.

Project: Sailing the Seas

Intaglio carving projects can be intricate with multiple designs or simple scenes. If you are carving a scene, then the elements closest to the forefront has to be carved the deepest. Aspects that are further into the background will be shallow or not carved at all since intaglio is a reverse carving technique. Any softwood measuring 8" x 6" x 1/" works for this project.

1. Draw a sailing scene onto the wood. Start by drawing a shoreline in the lower quarter of the wood, then add some sand dunes or mountains slightly above that. Draw a sailboat in the middle of the block so that it meets the shoreline. The picture can be as easy or difficult as you like but include at least two sails. The front of the sailboat should point towards the left edge of the piece of wood.

2. The item furthest away from the viewer is the land between the shore and sky, so start your intaglio

design by carving away between these two lines using a wide gouge. Only remove the top layer of the wood.

3. Use a very thin gouge to emphasize the shoreline by cutting a slightly deeper trough. Next, give texture to the water by removing a thin layer of wood using a wide gouge. Vary the depth of your cuts to create the effect of moving water.

4. Redraw the boat on your wood; if some of it has been shaved off then start carving the deck of the sailboat. The bowline should be left intact but use a thin gouge to remove enough wood from the hull. Make deeper cuts towards the front of the boat as it is closer to the viewer. Add a deep v-cut where the waterline meets the boat.

5. Carve a deep angled outline around the left-side sail, then use different size gouges to create depth in the sail. Do the same with the right-hand sail but make the carving slightly shallower, as it is further into the background.

6. Make a v-cut mast using a thin gouge or veiner.

7. Add any other details you want to the scene. Try making a globe cut sun or adding trees in the background. Once you are done, sand the piece and finish it according to your preferences.

Relief Carving

Relief carving is a technique whereby a thick slab of wood is carved to reveal a three-dimensional scene with a flat background. It is the opposite technique to intaglio that creates an image towards the inside of the wood. The final design of relief carving generates a protruding scene, which produces an illusion of dimension through shadows. Relief carving is one of the most beautiful techniques that most woodcarvers want to master. Ancient Egypt and Greece produced many relief carving masterpieces that depict the history of the nation.

There are several relief styles that a carver can choose between to produce an artwork. *High relief* pieces create dramatic visuals as the piece is carved with a depth of ½" to 2", which takes an extremely long time to carve. A variation of this style is *deep relief carving* where the carving is deeper than 2", but you need a wood slab that is double that thickness to avoid warping. *Low relief* pieces have a depth of less than ½" making it a trickier carve as lots of details have to go into a shallower design. One technique used in low relief (sometimes called bas) is leveling, such as when a flower is in front of a leaf. Pierced relief carving is an intricate style where small holes are pierced through the wood to create additional visual depth.

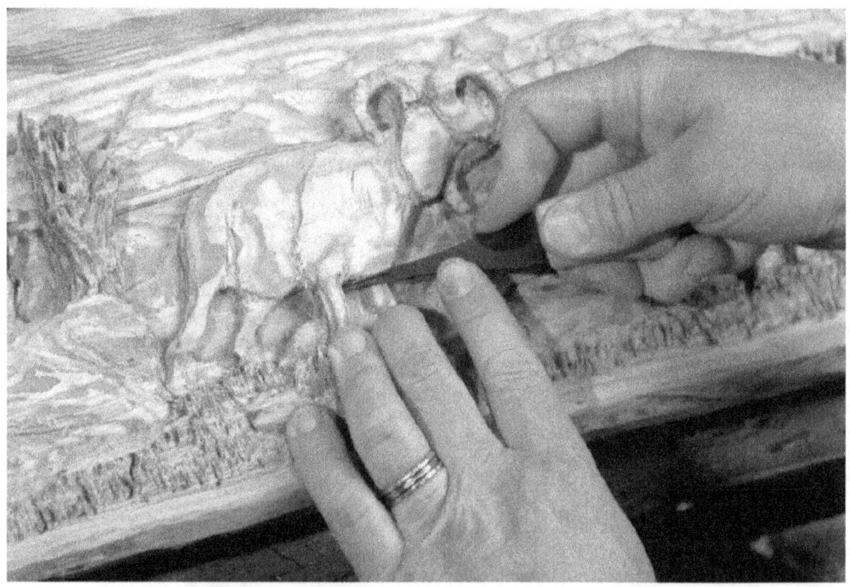

All relief carving pieces have distinct stages to complete the artwork. First, prepare a suitable slab of wood by sanding and cleaning the surface. Second, obtain a pattern or draw one yourself and transfer it onto the panel. Third, outline the main design by making incised cuts around key features and removing some of the surrounding wood. Fourth, remove any unwanted background material or enhance the areas around your main projects by deepening the cuts. Next, model the main design by adding additional features in finer detail. Finally, tidy up the background by removing any additional wood, if necessary, and apply a suitable finish.

Essential Tools

Chisels, gouges, and mallets are the main tools necessary for relief carving. The wider your range of tools, the more detail you can add to your artwork, so try to add equipment when possible. Additionally, a variety of tools makes carving easier and faster, as you do not have to go over the same area multiple times. A good rubber mallet is essential for carving deeper sections, as few people have enough power to drive a chisel through the wood on its own.

Secret Five: Relief carving is not as difficult as other people may have told you... if you use the correct tools.

The type of wood you use does affect your carving too. Any wood can work for relief carving, but let your design lead your choice. Softer woods like butternut, pine, and basswood remain popular options. However, relief carving seldom uses very long strokes due to the high level of detail, so you can select a harder wood. Keep in mind that harder woods are more challenging to carve and not suitable for beginner relief carvers. Mahogany or Black Ash is ideal if you want a challenge but these woods can chip and tear if you are not confident in your strokes.

Relief Cuts

Relief cutting is a technique that uses several cuts made by specific tools for a set purpose. There are three basic cuts, two technical cuts, and the v-cut. You can make the v-cut using either the traditional whittling method or use a veiner tool.

- *Back up chisel cut*: This basic cut is made by using the thin side of the chisel to add finer details.

- *Back down chisel cut*: Another basic cut, use the back, thicker part of the chisel to make a thicker cut into the wood.

- *Gouge cut*: The final basic cut is used to create round areas on the piece or shave excess wood from the background.

- *Undercut*: As a technical cut, the undercut features in high relief work and underneath the main feature. The viewer cannot see these cuts, but they add shadow and depth, which provides additional detail.

- *Stop cut*: This technical cut has the same purpose as other stop cuts: to end a cut. For relief carving, use a chisel to cut into the wood making a stopping point, and then carve towards this point.

Project: Alphabet

Relief carving may seem daunting at first but it becomes manageable once you start practicing. Start with a simple project where you can practice the basic stages of relief cutting but without too much detail. The alphabet, or a specific letter, in this case, is a great place to start. Use a 10" x 7" x ½" piece of softwood and keep your gouges, chisels, and mallet ready. Just as with incised carving, you may want to use a depth gauge for added precision.

1. Prepare your wood by ensuring it is clean then transfer a letter pattern to the wood. You can use any letter of your choosing and try this project several times with other letters until you master the technique. If you want to go very basic, then start with the "I". However, I would suggest going for "B" or "P" as they contain roundings and internal relief carving.

2. Turn the wood onto its side and mark a ⅓" all around the sides, so that you have a gauge for how deep you want to carve. For this letter, you will keep the letter raised from the wood and carve away everything along the outside, so markings on the side can assist in estimating depth.

3. Define the edge of the letter by making v-cuts using a low-angle grip just outside of the outline. This process acts as a stop cut for the letter and is sometimes called lining in.

4. Remove excess background material by using a gouge and making long strokes. Move from the edge of the wood towards the letter as it requires more control, but do not let the knife hit the letter. You want to remove all the wood up to the marking line that was made around the wood in step 2.

5. Focus on the tighter and internal areas next. Remove the wood inside the loop of the letter but work carefully so that you do not ruin your piece. Always work towards the v-cut but never remove material that is lower than the stop cut.

6. Place a flat or rounded chisel (depending on the outline) onto the outline at the top left of the letter. Hit the tool lightly with the mallet, so that it forms a crisp cut that ends in the stopping cut. Do this all around the letter paying particular attention to defining corners and curves.

7. Smooth the edge of the letter by running a flat chisel or blade around while applying consistent pressure and remove any stray wood chips.

8. Finish the background by using flatter chisels in a low grip to remove any ridges. Sand the letter to ensure it is smooth and equalize the background. Apply a wax, varnish, or other finish.

There you have it - four techniques to add to your wood carving skill set. After practicing these four techniques, you can call yourself an intermediate whittler with a range of abilities and new projects begging for your attention. These extra techniques make it possible to create more elaborate pieces regardless of whether you carve for fun or for a side income. I think it is a great idea to sell some of your pieces, as you cannot keep all your work and it generates an income to buy new tools!

Chapter 3:
Upgrade Your Tools

The basic carving techniques do not require a lot of tools. For whittling, there are four main types of knives, namely, a pocket knife, a flat steel blade, a hook knife, and the raindrop razor edge. However, having additional tools makes wood carving easier and we already saw that some woodcarving techniques require other tools.

None of the tools mentioned in this chapter are specialized tools, since they apply to almost all wood carving techniques. Having the right tool not only makes carving easier but also places less pressure on your hands. Take some time to practice with a variety of tools and identify where they hurt you. Wrap some leather around those sections or use an ergonomic handle so that you can work comfortably.

Secret Six: Ensure you hold and handle tools in the right way, especially carving knives. A grip that is too tight is just as dangerous and damaging as a grip that is too loose.

Knives

The basic wood carving tool is a knife. Most people start with a simple pocket knife for whittling and later purchase additional knives for detail work or for hollowing out items such as spoons. A flat-bladed knife works well for making broad strokes but a detail knife with a thin taper, like a raindrop razor edge, makes it easier to add definition to your carving. Yet, new techniques may necessitate additional knives.

Chip Carving Knives

Chip carving requires a different type of knife than other techniques. Specifically, you need a chip carving knife created especially for this purpose. A chip carving knife has a shorter blade, often made from durable carbon steel, with an ergonomic grip to reduce strain on your hands and wrists. The blades are thin making it easier to cut into the wood and create precision cuts into corners or at different angles.

Chip carving knives are available as single units or as a set and most are priced reasonably. If this is your first purchase, then save up for a set of knives (usually three per pack) that offer a variety of blades. Popular blade shapes include an angled flat steel blade that works well for straight wall cuts, blades with a rounded back for shaping more easily, and blades that end in a thin, sharp point making it easier to cut into the corners or make triangular cuts.

Some carvers believe that whittling should only be done with a pocket knife but it is not the case with chip carving. A chip carving knife is a recommendation for this technique because the blade of pocket knives are too thick and have a rounder nose. Additionally, a pocket knife's blade is weaker than the blade of a chip carving knife and there is a risk that you could snap your pocket knife. Although a pocket knife is useful and can work for chip carving, the correct knife produces better results.

Stab Knives

A stab knife is necessary for straight lines and accents. The blade has an extremely sharp, straight edge that glides into the wood without much effort. Usually, a stab knife has an angled blade of about 45 degrees that assists in creating depth. Place the blade of the stab knife perpendicular to the wood and push it into the piece. Control your knife carefully; it is not necessary to stab the wood with force.

Stab knives come in many materials. Most blades are made from stainless or carbon steel, while the handles are either wood or resin. Some stab knives have notches on the handle, which helps you remember how you held the knife for a specific cut. Since most of the blade cuts into the wood at once, the blade must be kept sharp at all times.

Detail Knives

The name of this knife explains its intended purpose. Detail knives are used to add fine details and definition to the artwork. Most detail knives have a sharp pointed end to get into all the little corners of the cut. Use this knife to sharpen the features of a chip cut, intaglio design, and especially, to carve features using the relief carving technique.

Detail knives come in a variety of shapes and sizes so choose one that works for your application. Many people have a few detail knives, such as the basic raindrop razor edge for a start. A short blade reduces the distance between your hand and the wood, which gives greater control and accurate carving. However, a longer blade may help if you have a deeper cut that requires detailing.

Hook Knives

Carving straight edges is quite a straightforward exercise, but hollowing out wood with a straight blade is a major challenge. Luckily, hook knives save the day and make it easier to hollow out spoons, bowls, and other designs. A hook knife looks exactly as the name suggests: the blade is curved into the shape of a hook. Most whittlers own at least one hook knife, as it is an invaluable tool.

A wide variety of hook knives are available on the market. Select your hook knife carefully because the cheaper ones usually do not last long. Yet, many woodcarvers want more than one hook knife, as the blades differ in many ways. The curvature of the hook can be narrow or wide. A narrow hook produces smaller shavings, while the wider hooks have a greater surface area to create shallow cuts. The hook may end in a sharp point for deep cutting or have a flat edge that generates a rounder effect. Additionally, the blade of the hook knife can be sharp on one side or both. With this range of features, it makes it challenging to choose just one. A great strategy for increasing your hook knife collection is to purchase the knife only if your project requires one.

Chisels

Hardwoods, deep relief cutting, and chip carving may benefit from the use of chisels. A chisel is a steel rod with a differentiating tip for various purposes. Chipping wood and removing small shavings at angles are the main use for chisels, which make them a standard part of the wood worker's toolbox. Some chisels come with a definitive handle or have a handle that fits several separate tools. However, some chisels consist of only the steel shaft and have no ergonomic handle in any fashion.

The lack of handle and thicker blade makes it difficult to use just your own force to create a cut. Rather, the chisel is placed into the correct position and then hit with a mallet at the end of the shaft, which catapults the chisel into the wood. Chisels have many purposes besides word work and may be used in carving other materials or in DIY and building activities. Ensure your chisels are suitable for woodwork and keep your wood chisels separate from other tools so that you do not ruin the blade through improper use. Besides the chisels listed below, there are other shapes such as tooth and point chisels.

Flat Chisel

A flat chisel has a 6" to 10" shaft that ends in a sharp, flat edge. The perpendicular cutting edge is suitable for creating straight lines, such as borders. The flat cutting edge can vary in length with some as narrow as ⅛" and others widening to 4". Check that your chisel has a sharpened edge that creates a bevel, otherwise it might not cut into the wood.

Hold a flat chisel perpendicular to the wood for a definite stop cut or place it at an angle for a v-cut. This shape assists in creating curves, shaping the basic outline, and removing excess wood. A flat chisel leaves very few ridges when used correctly, so work carefully and save time.

Skew Chisel

The skew chisel has a slanted blade rather than a flat edge. The blades are available at various angles, which makes for deeper or shallower carving. It works well for chip and relief carving where the depth of the incision varies across the cut. The toe is the longest part of the angled blade, while the shorter section is known as a heel. Be careful when using a skew chisel as the toe can lodge deeper into the wood than the heel making it difficult to remove the chisel once being hit with a mallet.

Fishtail Chisel

A fishtail chisel is a type of flat chisel but the end shape is slightly different. The edge of the blade flares out towards both sides, which creates a shape going from thin at the base of the shaft to wide at the cutting edge. The fishtail shape makes it easier to work in small spaces as you can maneuver the chisel into the correct area and angle.

Secret Seven: Learn about the gouges of your chisels. The gouge represents the shape and size of your chisel blade. Do not confuse a chisel with a gouging tool. Ultimately, the blade's size and curvature matter a lot, as they determine the structure of the cut.

Gouges

A gouge tool removes slivers of woods and small clumps in hard to reach areas. Do not confuse a gouge with a gauge. A gouge is a cutting tool, while a gauge is a measuring tool. Gouges look like a combination between a knife and a chisel. Most people consider a gouge to be a chisel with a thin, curved blade and secure handle. Many gouge tools can be used just by applying force from your body; however, a light mallet tap can assist the blade if the wood is very hard.

Three Basic Cuts

Gouges and knives make similar cuts in wood. Yet, there are times that a knife doesn't do a cut justice and you need a better tool. Oftentimes, a gouge is a more versatile choice. Three basic cuts set gouge tools apart from knives and make them with the extra expense.

The first type makes a channel in the shape of a concave cut. Secondly, turning the blade 180 degrees allows you to make a convex cut with rounded wood at the top of the cut. Finally, gouges make plunge cuts when the gouge is pushed into the wood in an effort to make a stop cut (Ellenwood, 2008, p. 121). Achieving these shapes with a knife is challenging, takes a lot of time, and you have no guarantee that you will achieve the desired effect. Investing in gouges is a sensible choice, so look for a durable set with a variety of tools.

Size and Sweep

Manufacturers use the terms *size* and *sweep* to differentiate between gouges. The size of the blade is found by measuring the gouge across its width. Measure the blade at its widest part, but note that gouge' sizes are mostly given in metric units rather than inches. Check your set carefully to see which system was used by the manufacturer. Gouges come in many sizes from ⅛" to 1" providing several options for your carving.

The sweep of a gouge refers to curvature in the blade. Although there are slight variations between manufacturers, the definition of the sweep remains the same. A number (#) designates the sweep and ranges from #2 to #11, where a higher number indicates a deeper curve. Shallow gouges range between #2 and #4, medium-depth gouges are #5 to #7, deep gages include while #8 and #9. The deepest gouges are #10 and #11 and create thin, deep lines, similar to those made by veiners.

Clearly, there are many gouge tools when considering the sweep and size combinations. Yet, you do not need one in every size and depth. Purchase a thin and wider gouge within each sweep category as an initial set, then buy additional gouges when you can. Although size matters, the sweep is not precise, so there is leeway when following design instructions. For example, a #6 or #8 tool is suitable if the project requires a #8 gouge.

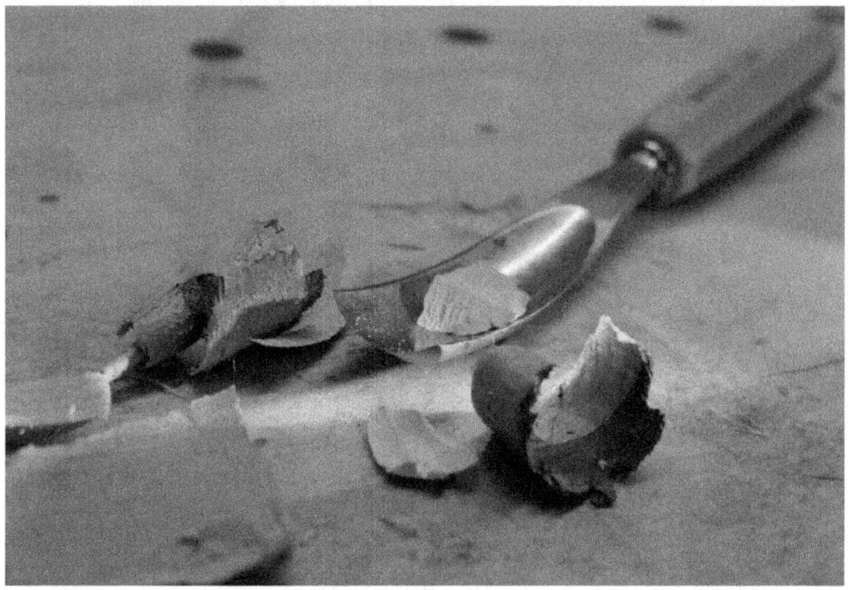

Spoon Gouge

A spoon gouge looks like a combination of a gouge and a hook knife. The general shape is similar to a spoon, which makes it easier to create a hollow in the wood. The curve at the end of the gouge is very short and tapers to a sharp blade so that you can get into tight corners. Additionally, turning the gouge around allows you to cut into the wood at an almost perpendicular angle.

V-Type Gouge

V-type gouges have an angled blade creating a "v" rather than a fluid curve. The size of the tool is measured as the widest part between the two edges, which are called wings in wood carving terms. Rather than having a numbered sweep, a v-tool comes with a specific angle made by the two blades. The most common v-tools have 45, 60, or 90-degree angles, although there are other options. A unique extension of this tool is a winged-v gouge that cuts a "v" while creating convex roundings along the side.

U-Type

A u-type gouge produces a trough with deeper sides than the traditional gouges. It is quite easy to confuse the two since the shapes are similar. U-type gouges are essential when making deep relief carving pieces, as you can remove more wood in less time. The shape is much more of an ellipse than a circle, so do not use this gouge for globe cuts.

Veiners

Veiners cut thin channels into the wood, just like the veins in your body. Use a veiner for fine details and features, such as deep cuts, outlines, and hair. Some confusion exists regarding veiners because they look a lot like gouges; however, there is no strict definition in this regard. A #11 gouge is the same size as a veiner. When comparing a #10 gouge with a veiner, you will see the wings of the veiner are higher making the cuts deeper than a gouge tool (Ellenwood, 2008, p. 122). Still, most people refer to this tool as a veiner, as it is easier to know what a person is talking about. A #11 veiner is an essential tool for all intermediate woodcarvers.

V-Tools

The v-tool, also known as a parting tool, has a blade with a distinct "v" shape for angular cutting. A v-tool helps in making outlines, undercuts, texture, and unique details. Some people believe that joining two chisel blades creates the v-tool but it is more complex than this simple definition. The difference between a v-tool and a v-gouge is the shape of the cut. The v-gouge creates a valley since it has a slight curvature in the sides, while the shape of the v-tools produces a wall as the blades are straight. V-tools come in various angles with the most popular options being 30, 45, 60, and 90 degrees. The smaller the angle between the blades, the thinner the line, so some manufacturers offer 24-degree v-tools for super fine lines.

Intermediate wood carving techniques require additional tools since you are expanding your skillset from just whittling. Build up your tool collection slowly and only purchase a tool if you need it for a project. Keep your tools in good condition by cleaning them thoroughly after every use. Sharpen the blades and store the tools properly, so that they last for a long time. Besides these tools, you might consider adding extra accessories to your workshop.

Chapter 4:
Accessorize Your Workshop

Accessories and other tools add value to your workshop and make your work a breeze. The tools in this chapter are not primary wood carving tools but some of them are useful in woodworking and improve the carving process. You might have these tools in your collection already or make purchases as you need the tools.

Secret Eight: Hobbycraft stores create the perception that you need an abundance of tools when carving a masterpiece. But, you don't. A select few essentials will suffice, but you might carve more easily with some optional tools. Everything you need is specified in this book.

Carving Mallet

Carving mallets are essential when working with chisels and sometimes for gouges, as they provide the force to move the tool through the wood. Mallets stocked at hardware stores come in a variety of shapes, sizes, and materials including metal, wood, and rubber. Metal and heavy mallets are not ideal for woodwork as their hardness may damage the tool you are hitting. A wood or light rubber mallet is preferable for carving, although some hobby shops stock mallets made for woodworking specifically. Some people turn their own wooden mallets from wood, which is a nice project for yourself, or ask a friend with a lathe to make one for you.

Mallets assist in moving tools through a medium, in this case, wood. The advantage of mallets lies in the strength with which you swing it, which gives great control. The harder you strike the complementary tool, the deeper the tool drives into the wood, while hitting it softer generates less movement. Always clamp the wood to a workbench when using a mallet, as the force can move the wood across the table (Ellenwood, 2008, p. 162).

Secret Nine: Ensure you use a light mallet (or hammer) as much as possible. Using a heavier mallet can cause muscle strain, especially when using them improperly or if you do not know the basic technique. Never swing the mallet from your elbow; always use a swinging action coming from your shoulder.

There are many types of woodworking mallets, so select one (or several) suitable for your intentions. A bench mallet is a large tool made from wood with angled sides that work well for driving tools into stubborn wood. The flatter sides on the width of the bench mallet work well when you require less pressure. A less familiar option is the carver's mallet that comes in three sizes and a variety of applications. The carver's mallet is unique as it does not have an angular head but has a distinctive bell-like shape. Use a larger carver's mallet with a chisel or gouge to remove a lot of background material without experiencing fatigue, or select a smaller one for light, precision work. Another variation is a brass carver's mallet, which has a wooden handle and a small, brass head. This mallet is ideal for precision carving with more weight and in small spaces.

Files

Files are a controversial tool in the wood carving community as purists believe these tools provide artificial finishing. However, modern carvers may find files as a useful accessory to finish work, especially when you want a smooth surface rather than ridges or textures. Files help in shaping the wood and smoothing the surface by removing small slivers and stray pieces. Using files for initial rough finishing often works faster than using sandpaper, although you still need to sand your piece for a pristine finish.

Each file has three distinct parts, namely, the length, tang, and heel. The file's length is the cutting area, which has teeth on it for filing. Larger teeth create a coarser surface while smaller, closely packed teeth make for a finer filing surface. The smoother and slightly tapering section between the length and tang is called the heel. The tang is an area at the end of the file, which is usually tapering and thinner. Note that a handle must be placed over the tang, as it is not a handle in itself. Most files come without a handle since one interchangeable handle can be used for all files.

File types are a reference to the cutting surface of the file and determine the abrasiveness. Use a single-cut file for precision work. A double-cut and coarse file removes wood quickly, while bastard and second files remove less wood and at a slower pace. The smooth type removes wood very slowly and leaves a smooth surface, which is ready for sanding.

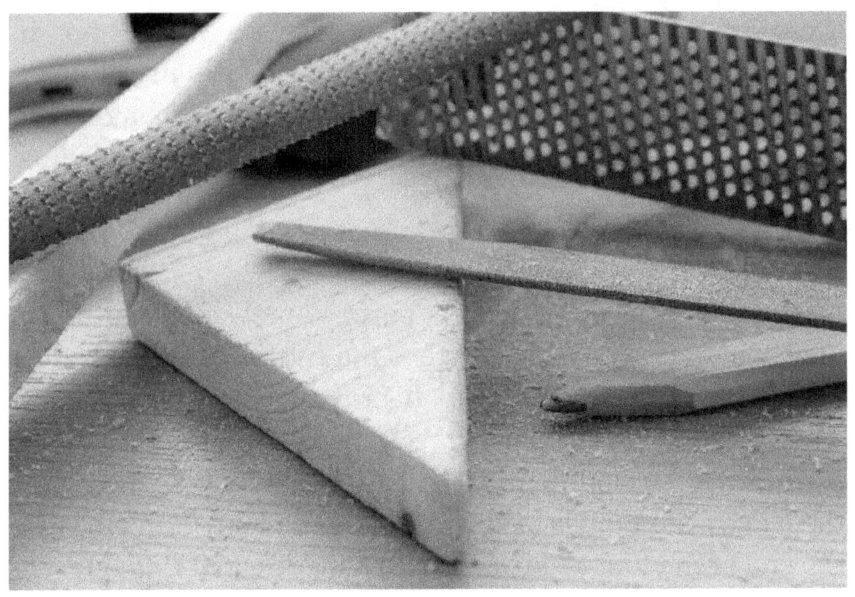

There are many file shapes called profiles. Each one has a specific application but you do not need a file of every type and size. The profile, or shape of the length, determines the use of the file. Basic file profiles include rectangular, semi-circle, triangular, round, square, and tapered shapes that fit into a variety of spaces. Remember that files can clog with frequent use and become dirty, so clean them after use with a nylon brush. Store them away from moisture to avoid damage and apply chalk before use to discourage clogging.

Rasps

A rasp is a very coarse type of file that removes wood quickly. Rather than planing the surface, rasps scrape away at the top layer and leave a rough surface for further finishing. The length of a rasp contains triangular teeth, arranged randomly for faster working. The larger sized teeth prevent clogging as wood slivers fall out while using a rasp. A smaller variety of rasps exists because they are not used for precision work.

Needle Files

Needle files are thin, smaller sized files, which come in many profiles. These files are the right tool for precise filing and have a second cut surface for a smoother finish. Most hardware and hobby craft stores sell needle files in a set of twelve with an interchangeable handle.

Rifflers

Rifflers are smaller files but have a file length on both ends in different sizes. It does not have a handle but the middle section of the file has an area for easier gripping. The filing ends are available in several profiles with most tools having the same profile on both ends although one side will be smaller than the other. Popular shapes include knife, round, curve, triangle, square, and straight ends, among others. Rifflers can fit into tight working areas, which make them ideal for relief work.

Microplanes

A microplane is a very coarse file, similar to a cheese grater's finest place. Microplanes have curved or flat blades and contain small holes throughout the length to remove wood slivers rapidly. Be careful when using a microplane as you can hurt yourself easily. Microplanes are ideal for removing large areas of wood stock like backgrounds in relief carving.

Filing Styles

Many people just grab a file and get going but filing incorrectly can damage the wood and ruin your hard work. Use one of the following two styles for filing to finish your work properly. These filing styles assist in treating the wood properly and makes final finishing easier.

The first style is draw filing to finish a piece. Hold the handle with one hand and the tip of the file with the other hand and place the file perpendicular to the wood. Push the file across the wood surface using very little pressure. Too much pressure may remove wood excessively and create additional hollow areas. The teeth only file on the forward, pushing stroke, so remove the file from the wood surface and start again, rather than pulling it back across the wood.

Cross filing is the second style and helps in removing rougher areas of wood. Place the file at an angle to the wood while holding both ends of the file and run it across the wood with medium pressure. Never place the file flat and straight across the wood as it has too much friction. Insufficient pressure results in the file skipping over the wood causing irreparable damage. Always use a diagonal stroke when filing across the grain to avoid wood tears and splitting.

Clamping Devices

In whittling, you hold the wood with your hands and sometimes support it against another surface. The new techniques require you to use both hands while carving, such as holding a chisel in one hand and a mallet in the other, making it difficult to keep the wood stable. A piece of wood moving across the table (sometimes called walking) is detrimental and can ruin your piece entirely. However, the force applied is highly likely to move the wood, so you need to hold it in place with some type of clamp.

There are many types of clamps so find some that work for you and the project you are working on. An oddly-shaped project and the hardness of the wood determine the best clamp for the job as you have to secure it properly without damaging the wood. Clamps also assist in holding wood pieces together when you create joins or add glued elements onto the wood.

Carver's Vise

A vise is a holding tool that attaches to the workbench for extra stability. Vises move along several dimensions, although traditional workshop vises only have two plates that move apart. A carver's vise has additional clamping areas to ensure a piece is properly secured for carving. The best vise option is one that moves in all three dimensions as you have a wider range of clamping options. Do some research before purchasing a carver's vise, as you want one that clasps properly and has a gripping mounting plate. The vise and wood being held should not slip even when using a mallet.

Carver's Arm

The carver's arm is an extension of the vise and provides additional mobility for woodcarvers. The tool looks like a human arm and has a hinge joint that bends in the direction you want, which is usually up and down positions. Some carver's arms include a separate screw at the arm's end for side-to-side movement. The vertical and horizontal movement makes the carver's arm a desirable tool that eases the strain on the hands. Maple wood is a popular choice for carver's arms as it is strong and does not hurt the piece it is holding. Although carver's arms are reasonably priced, you can find instructions online to make your own one.

Machinist's Vise

A machinist's vise is the traditional workbench vise with a set of jaws that can be opened and closed along a set range. The plates on the inside of the jaw are metal and may have serrated areas, which may damage the wood while clamping. However, you want to secure the wood properly to avoid slippage when hitting a tool with a mallet. The best way to protect your wood and secure it tightly is to place a piece of softwood on each side of your work so that the vise's plates press against the spare blocks rather than directly against the carving piece. Alternatively, some hardware and woodcraft stores sell protective pads that attach to the plates by a magnet and provide cushioning for the wood being held.

Alligator Clips

An alligator clip is a long, pointed clamp that looks similar to an alligator's jaw and has a few serrated teeth. These clips are used for more than just wood and are often found at the end of cables, such as those at the end of vehicle jump-starting cables. However, alligator clips are a lot smaller and come in various sizes so you can select clips that fit your piece. Keep in mind that the serrated jaw may bite into the wood, especially softwoods, so attach the clips in areas that will be finished or removed later on. Many carvers secure alligator clips to rods and a table weight, which enables the piece to be held midair and makes it easier to work all around. Alligator clips can slip so secure them properly and do not use force on the wood as it can dislodge the piece.

Web Clamp

A web clamp is made by wrapping a ratchet strap around the wood. A ratchet strap, made from nylon, has a ratchet end that pulls the strap taut and keeps the piece together tightly. Ratchet straps are mainly used for joining pieces of wood or holding glued elements onto the wood so that they attach properly. A web clamp is effective and easy to use but has a lot more strength than you may think once pulled taut. Never place the ratchet area directly against the wood as it can scratch away at the surface; rather, keep it in the open area of the web. Additionally, check that the straps do not cut into the wood and cause unnecessary damage. Add a small block of softwood between the nylon strap and working piece for additional protection but check that the block does not slip while tightening the ratchet strap.

Rubber Bands

Rubber bands work well to hold wood that has odd shapes. Most clamping devices are made to hold wood pieces that are of a particular size or shape, usually with flat or rectangular surfaces. However, many whittling and wood carving pieces are not angular at all and have three-dimensional objects or rounded edges. Clamping these pieces in traditional clamps is very challenging and an item that slips can experience damage that ruins your hard work. In these cases, rubber bands are the best options as they hold the wood securely even when it is a strange shape. Opt for a wider rubber band that won't cut into the pieces instead of thin office-type rubber bands. Check that the rubber bands are in good condition before using them and discard any band that has cracks or dry spots as they may snap while holding the piece.

C, Spring, Quick-Change, and Toggle Clamps

A variety of shaped clamps holds wood to a workbench or assists in joining pieces of wood together. These clamps get their names from their shape or clamping mechanism. Many types exist, and these four are some of the most popular options, but you can use any type that you prefer or have available in your workshop.

C-clamps secure wood panels to the workbench so that it does not move during the carving process. Sizes range between 1" and 12" so use clamps that correspond to the size of your work. Using a too large clamp makes it prone to movement or slipping when pushed by hand while a clamp that is too small cannot hold the piece securely. C-clamps require manual manipulation to open and close, and tightening them can be a time-consuming process, especially when you need to clamp the work quickly.

A spring clamp is an automatic clamp that opens and closes quickly. The tips pressing against the wood and handles have a polyvinyl coating to decrease the chance of damage. A variety of sizes are available including mini-clamps and larger options up to 4". Spring clamps are especially useful when you need to create a good bond between glued objects as they apply sufficient pressure on the items.

Another alternative is the quick-change clamp that has a user-friendly mechanism. Slide the jaws onto the sides of the wood then tighten the grip by squeezing the pistol. A trigger releases the jaws when you are ready to remove the wood. All of these actions can be done by using only one hand, so a quick change clamp is perfect when you have to hold onto the wood while grabbing a clamp quickly. The jaws of quick-change clamps usually have a soft coating for added protection. However, the pressure applied by the jaws is not strong enough to glue pieces of wood together and the wood may move if you apply a heavier mallet blow.

Toggle clamps are another option for holding projects. These clamps have a lever handle and rubber tip that locks the wood into place. The rubber coating protects the wood from damage, but the clamp might be in your way while working on the piece. Attaching the clamp to the wood is easy, as you only need to pull the handle up or push it down and it secures itself.

Bar and Pipe Clamps

Bar and pipe clamps have been around for generations to hold longer objects securely. Most consist of a long shaft that has a fixed head and a tail that slides along the device. Traditionally, a bar clamp has a rectangular steel shaft to which the head and tail connects, although there are some differences in design. A pipe clamp is similar but fits onto any length of ¾" threaded pipe. With a pipe clamp, the head is screwed into place while the tail slides along the pipe and has a disc clutch for holding purposes.

Bar and pipe clamps come in lengths ranging from 4" to 6 feet, so they are a versatile tool for holding small or large projects. Some of these clamps now feature fast action sections that secure the wood quickly and easily. Find an option that works best for the size of your design and check that the jaws do not damage the wood when clamping. These clamps are ideal when carving figurines, totem poles, and three-dimensional pieces.

Numerous tools and accessories can enhance your wood carving experience. These tools are not essential but make it easier to hold your pieces and assist in finishing projects beautifully. While these additional tools are a great extension to carving equipment, you also need proper wood to create a masterpiece.

Chapter 5:
Know Your Wood

Comprehensive knowledge of wood, grain, and its behavior empowers a carver to select a suitable blank and carve a masterpiece. The more you know, the better your work and ability to use the wood. The basic anatomy of wood includes the crown, trunk, and roots.

Secret Ten: *Understanding the anatomy of wood and knowing the best wood type for different techniques is more important than owning many high-tech carving tools.*

The crown includes all the branches, twigs, limbs, and leaves. Through photosynthesis, the leaves produce food for the rest of the tree, which is called sap and transported throughout the tree. The trunk is the segment in between the crown and roots, which often is a wide, solid area, free of limbs. The roots anchor the tree and absorb minerals and water from the ground. The trunk is of most importance to carvers since it contains the best carving wood.

Parts of a Tree Trunk

The tree trunk is the large, upright area of the tree. From the trunk grows branches that support flowers, fruit, and leaves. Five layers make up the trunk of all trees, starting from the outer bark and moving towards the heartwood, which is the deepest layer. Each layer has a specific role and affects the usability of the wood, so get to know it and your work becomes better.

Outer Bark

On the very outside of the tree is the outer bark, which protects the trunk from external elements. The outer bark renews itself from inside the trunk so that the tree does not dry out in the heat or absorb excess moisture when it rains. It also provides insulation to extreme weather conditions and prevents insects from entering the wood.

Inner Bark

Also known as phloem, the inner bark transports food between the inside and outside of the tree and the leaves. The inner bark has a short lifespan but works hard during that time. Once it dies, the inner bark transforms into cork and changes to outer bark.

Cambium Cell Layer

The area below the inner bark is the cambium cell layer, which is the layer responsible for trunk growth. Responsible for new bark production, the cambium cell layer uses hormones, called auxins, from the inner bark to stimulate growth. Auxin production occurs when leaf buds start growing on tree branches, usually during Springtime.

The cambium cell layer, sometimes called sap, is the sticky liquid released from trees when they are cut. The time of year that a tree is cut determines the amount of liquid in the cell layer. During spring and summer, the cambium layer experiences rapid cell division making cuts very sticky and bark often fall from the tree as it does not have a good binding agent to the sapwood. During winter and fall, growth slows and fewer cells form in the cambium layer, which generates a tight bond between sapwood and bark. Some carving projects get aesthetic appeal when the bark remains intact during the carving process. If you want to try this method, then use a tree from a fall or winter harvest.

Sapwood

Sapwood is a softer and younger wood between the cambium cell layer and heartwood. The sapwood transports water from the roots to the branches and leaves. Sapwood fulfills this role for several years until it loses vitality when new rings are formed through growth. Sapwood has a lighter color than heartwood so it is easy to distinguish between the different layers.

Heartwood

Heartwood lies at the center (heart) of the tree and is the supporting structure for the rest of the tree. Technically, the heartwood is dead, but it remains strong and does not decay if the external layers are healthy. Heartwood is a composite material that contains hollow cellulose fibers held together by lignin, which is similar to glue. This composite material has exceptional strength and can support a lot of weight.

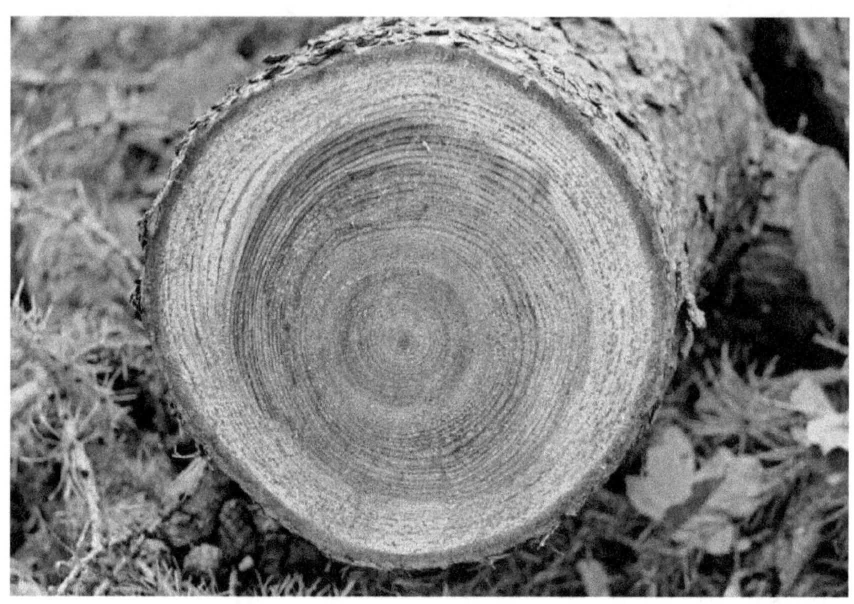

Understanding Wood Behavior

Besides the original five layers, wood has other characteristics that dictate its usability and behavior. The qualities are internal to the wood and cannot be seen without making a cross-section into the tree. However, these attributes are visible once the trunk is cut.

Pith

The pith is found right in the middle of the tree and becomes visible in the trunk. It is the oldest part of the tree and referred to as juvenile wood. The pith has some inherent weaknesses that cause it to crack easily, which may extend to the rest of the wood if it dries out or becomes vulnerable. Most carvers do not use the pith area in their work as it is brittle. If your wood does have a pith, then position the design to avoid the pith or keep it away from view.

Annual Rings

Annual rings are a growth indicator for trees that start around the pith and move all the way to the exterior of the wood. The rings contain two parts known as spring or earlywood, and summer or latewood. Active growth occurs during the growing season and forms the earlywood, which has thin walls and large cells. Growth decreases throughout the season, creating thicker walls with smaller cells, known as latewood. A higher concentration of cellulose gives latewood a darker color. These two parts create a definite ring for each year of growth with varying width dependent on growing conditions.

Vessels and Rays

Vessels and rays are the circulatory systems of trees that transport substances throughout the wood. Vessels run vertically through the tree and appear as small holes when a cross-section of wood is placed under a microscope. The vessels are responsible for transporting minerals and water from the roots to the leaves. Rays run horizontal to the tree and appear as lines under a microscope. During photosynthesis, the sap produced is sent to the rest of the wood through these rays. Vascular rays have thinner cell walls and weave around the vessels to bond them together.

Even though vessels and rays require a microscope to be seen properly, they have a big impact on wood behavior. Sometimes, a gouge or knife enters an area between vessels and tears the ray cells apart, which splits the vessels. This issue is known as "splitting with the grain" and creates tears in the wood. Cutting across the grain is a better option since you do not cut into the vessels. These potential problems emphasize the importance of grain familiarity with cutting.

Wood Grain

Wood grain is a term used to describe the appearance, texture, and alignment of wood fibers. Fibers are long thin cells that grow in a certain direction to create alignment with other cells. The grain is visible when you cut into the wood but you need additional information to use this identification for proper wood carving practices.

Grain texture refers to the cell arrangement, size, and variation, which create either fine or coarse grain. As the wood dries out, the vessels become empty and form pores, which are a distinguishing element between soft and hardwood. Softwood has densely packed fibers, while large pores in hardwood make them difficult to carve. Closed grain wood has very small pores that are difficult to see, while wood with large pores is known as open grain. Carving wood may be susceptible to tears if the pores are large.

The grain orientation creates a pattern known as figure grain, which is used in some projects. There are four types of grain patterns that are important for woodcarvers. A *straight grain* block of wood has a grain that runs in only one direction throughout the wood. When cell growth extends from the tree center, the pattern is known as *cross-grain*. Sometimes, a tree trunk twists over many years of growth, which creates a *spiral-grain*. Finally, *interlocked grain* patterns occur when twists in the trunk force fibers into different areas causing misalignment.

Figure grain has qualities that differentiate cuts and wood from each other because vessels and rays grew uniquely. *Silver grain* is seen when some types of trees are sawn in a specific way to reveal prominent rays. Using a wood cutting from a section where branches and limbs meet creates a *crotch figure*. Sometimes, the vessels have a wavy growth pattern referred to as *curly grain*. *Bird's eye* grain is seen when layers of cells cause small dimples in the wood, while larger dimples result in *quilted figure* grain. However, dimples occur when a fungal infection affects the tree. A *ribbon figure* is seen when vessels change their direction after a few years of growth. Finally, the *burl figure* represents grain that caused a growth on the side of the tree in a swirling pattern.

Grain plays a role in every single cut made into the wood. Knowing the types of grain and how it behaves when applying tools is essential. When a tool enters the wood at the wrong angle, it can damage the wood and split the layers. Sometimes, the tool then becomes stuck in the wood, and extracting it causes further damage, while the tool may slip at other times and cut into the wrong area.

Working With The Grain

The grain assists in determining the direction of a cut and gives you an idea of any issues that may pop up during the process. The most important thing is to cut across the grain so that you do not split the vessels. However, most books, hobby craft stores, and internet searches suggest cutting with the grain, but that is exactly when splits occur.

Secret Eleven*: A common belief among carvers is that carving should occur along (or with) the wood grain. Wood splitting often occurs when carving along the grain. However, carving across the grain is easier, as you have better control over the pieces of wood being removed from the work.*

Two-grain cutting styles have been mentioned already but there are other cutting methods too. Cutting *across the grain* refers to cuts made perpendicular to vessels, while parallel cuts are typical of cutting *with the grain*. Another option is to cut the wood at an angle to the grain, which is known as cutting *against the grain*. When a person does cut into the grain, they make incisions between the vessels. However, this cut easily produces *splitting with the grain*, which tears the wood (Ellenwood, 2008, p. 67). Although most projects come with instructions on the best grain and cut to use, there are many instances where the wood you have available necessitates other forms of cutting. The type of wood also informs the cutting method for the best results.

Good Woods for Carving

Wood is classified into softwood and hardwood. Softwood is easier to carve than hardwood, which makes it ideal for whittling. Several softwood options were explored in the previous book, including basswood, balsa, butternut, pine, and a few others. This section presents woods suitable for intermediate carvers. They are a bit more challenging to use, but none of these woods are too hard to carve. Both cherry and maple wood is grown commercially in the United States and Canada, so they are readily accessible. The latter two options, mahogany, and tupelo are available here but they are not grown commercially. However, some woods feature these trees and timber yards may source them on request.

Cherry

Cherry wood comes from the Latin species known as *Prunus serotina*. The wood is moderately difficult to work with but is an attractive option because of its color. Cherry wood has rich reddish brown hues that look stunning when a clear coat of finish is applied after carving. The wood becomes darker as it ages, even during the drying process.

Carving fine details into cherry wood is possible, so you can use it to produce beautifully textured designs. Cherry wood is a popular choice for wood crafts and construction, which increases the price greatly. If you do go with cherry wood for your project, then practice your cuts on a cheaper wood before you start your main design to avoid ruining an expensive cut. Additionally, do not use power tools with cherry wood as it burns the surface. However, it is perfectly suitable for woodworking done by hand.

Maple

Maple wood is another popular carver's choice but you need some patience to produce a masterpiece. There are two types of maple trees for carving, namely, the *Acer saccharum,* which is a hard variety, and the softer *Acer rubrum,* which is ideal for carvers. Maple is reasonably priced and readily available at timber yards.

Figure grain is prevalent in maple and can add an aesthetic quality to your finished product. Just remember that grain patterns create carving challenges so you have to work carefully while carving maple, as the grain density changes throughout any wood segment. Some of the grain patterns seen in maple are curly, bird's eye, tiger, and fiddleback. The grain texture forces carvers to work carefully so maple lends itself well to highly detailed carvings. Finish your maple artwork by polishing the wood to a glossy shine.

Mahogany

Mahogany, with the Latin name *Swietenia macrophylla*, grows in many countries across the world although the greatest number come from Central America. It is sometimes called Honduras mahogany. A medium to coarse texture makes it a bit more challenging to carve, although the grain is relatively straight with few interlocked areas.

Mahogany is a great choice if you plan on having a natural-looking project since the color plays beautifully through the wood. The hues range from light to dark and include reddish-brown and rich, deep reds. This interplay of colors looks great in relief carving, for boxes, and larger projects that display the colors. Mahogany is used frequently for making furniture or decorative panels.

Tupelo

Tupelo is a type of black gum tree but the name is confusing because the wood's color is light. Tupelo has interlocked grain with a uniform texture, which does not split easily. It is a challenging wood to work with, as the grain is tight and varied, but the final result is rewarding for any carver. The color of Tupelo ranges from light to pale brown and may have patches with a gray hue. It takes various colors well, so try staining Tupelo as a finish.

When selecting wood, choose a piece that is large enough for your design but not too big that there is a lot of excess stock. Consider the grain pattern, colors, and finished product before you choose your blank. Ensure the wood is suitable for your application and that there are no inherent issues that weaken your finished product. Although wood is

your primary material, you can avoid damaging the wood by
keeping your tools sharp.

Chapter 6:
Know the Sharpening Stones

A sharp blade is important for wood carving activities. Razor-sharp blades slide through wood easily and require less force to move across or against the grain. Unwanted directional changes and cutting yourself occur when a blade is dull. So, prioritize sharpening your bladed tools.

Secret Twelve*: The right tools are important. But, using sharp tools is crucial. Improper tool care and not sharpening tools correctly using specific techniques with the right equipment causes problems. Replacing your tools becomes a frequent occurrence if your blades are dull and damaged due to incorrect or lack of maintenance. Additionally, your carving quality decreases as a dull knife causes damage.*

Detailed care keeps your tools in the best condition possible. Sharpening blades requires two distinct steps. Firstly, shape a proper cutting angle using a sharpening stone. Secondly, polish the blade for a razor-sharp edge (Ellenwood, 2008, p. 201). Another term for this process is honing, which means to sharpen and refine a blade.

Various sharpening stones are available including oil, diamond, water, ceramic, and Arkansas stones. Ellenwood suggests the pros and cons of these stones, as shown under each type of stone below (2008, p. 202-219). Each one has specific characteristics, so find one that works for your blades.

Oil Stones

Among the most popular sharpening tools, the oil stone is probably the one you are most familiar with. Oil stones are cut from various materials. Novaculite, commonly known as an Arkansas stone, is discussed later in this chapter. Other options include Aluminium Oxide and Silicon Carbide.

Aluminum Oxide is a man-made stone and a popular option for sharpening. Besides fast cutting, Aluminium Oxide stones assist in refining the edge. Usually orange or brown in color, the stones have grits titled coarse, medium, and fine. Yet, these stones are coarser than Arkansas stones. Use Aluminium Oxide stones for sharpening and then move to Arkansas stones for further detailing.

Silicone Carbide is another popular option, as it cuts the fastest of all oil stones. Silicone Carbide stones come in coarse, medium, and fine grits, but do not create a fine edge. The coarse nature of these stones makes them best for initial shaping and sharpening. It has a gray color. Silicone Carbide stones are available readily and inexpensive.

Swarf removal, commonly known as metal filing, requires additional oil on the stone during sharpening. Using oil can be messy, so have a dedicated work area for sharpening with oil stones. Always clean blades thoroughly after using oil stones to remove any residue, otherwise the oil transfers to the wood causing stains.

Pros:

- Reasonable pricing

- Relatively fast cutting

- Combination stones are available

- Require little maintenance

Cons:

- Finer grits not available

- Cups with repeated usage

- Oil transfer to blades results in wood staining

Diamond Stones

Diamond stones consist of a metal plate topped with tiny diamonds. These diamonds are either mono-crystalline or poly-crystalline, although the former is longer lasting and more desirable. Industrial-grade diamonds make up the surface, which creates a harder stone. As a result, you apply less pressure while achieving faster sharpening. The diamonds increase the price of these stones and make them very expensive. However, they last much longer than other stones, which equalizes the costs in the long-run.

Diamond stones come in two styles. The first type has small holes, sharpens quickly, and catches swarf in the crevices. The second type has an uninterrupted diamond surface, which does not catch swarf and is ideal for sharpening pointed tools. Both types of diamond stones are available in various grits. Sometimes, an extra coarse diamond stone is utilized when flattening water or oil stones.

Pros:

- Fastest cutting stone

- Available in various grits

- Flatness remains ±0.002 of an inch

- Requires less pressure

- Lower maintenance than other stones

- Works with honing oil, water, or dry

- Unbreakable

Cons:

- Expensive

- Lighter pressure requires a mental adjustment

Water Stones

Water stones use water in the sharpening process. Although both synthetic and natural water stones exist, natural stones are not easy to come by. Synthetic stones dominate the market as they are available more readily. Regardless of the material, water stones are a bit more expensive than some of the other options.

Aluminum Oxide is the main component of synthetic water stones. It is the same material used in some oil stones but the adhesives combining the material differ. Water stones sharpen blades quickly as they are soft and reveal a new cutting surface often. As the blade moves across the stone, it removes surface material. However, the new sharper surface creates unevenness and requires flattening for continuous use.

Available in numerous grits, water stones are suitable for shaping and polishing blades. Soaking the stone in water before use is mandatory, but never let it freeze as it causes permanent damage. Additionally, dry your tools properly after sharpening to avoid rust formation.

Pros:

- Available in a variety of grits (coarse to extra fine)

- Fast cutting

- A single stone set can hone, shape, and sharpen

- Fine and extra-fine grits work well for polishing

Cons:

- Slightly more expensive

- Coarse grits erode rapidly

- Requires frequent flattening

- Requires water soaking

- Water may cause rust on tools

- Freezing wet stones are an issue

Ceramic Stones

Ceramic stones are constructed from a ceramic material, usually clay or other earthly compounds. The construction of ceramic stones produces a hard surface, which does not require any fluids for cutting. Yet, some people achieve better results when adding a touch of fluid. These stones are available as either a rod or a block and range in grit from medium to ultra-fine.

A variation of this stone is the ceramic water stone. An adhesive binds the individual ceramic materials together, which require water for proper cutting. However, you do not need to soak a ceramic water stone. Just add some water during the sharpening process. Ceramic water stones are available in numerous grits that do not wear as easily as other water stones. They are durable and do not erode quickly.

Pros:

- Superfine grits available

- Durable wear

- Low maintenance with infrequent flattening

Cons:

- Expensive

- Delicate and brittle

- Slow cutting

- Only available in fine grits

Arkansas Stones

Arkansas stones are a naturally occurring type of oil stone. Quarried in Arkansas, these stones are shaped and graded in the United States. Arkansas stones use a mineral oil during sharpening, although some people use them as water stones but that requires additional care. Pores in the stone may clog up with swarf, so never use the stone dry. They range from soft to hard, with each stone having unique characteristics.

Arkansas stones come in various colors, which often correspond with their grit type. Rather than using grit, Arkansas stones have hardness and density gradings. A coarse stone is soft and less dense, with Soft Arkansas ranging in grit from 600-800. Although some people use only a coarse stone, it does leave some bite to the edge. Finer Arkansas stones are hard and very dense, which makes them ideal for honing blades. The Hard Arkansas stone has a grit between 800 - 1000, while 1200+ associates with Hard Translucent or Hard Black Arkansas stones.

Pros:

- Simultaneous polishing and sharpening

- Mirror-like finish

- Slower erosion

- Works best for final blade honing

- Natural stone obtainable in four grades

Cons:

- Expensive

- Slow cutting

- Only fine grits available

Sharpening stones come in many materials, each with distinct qualities. No right or wrong stone exists, so, select the stones that work best for your tools. Sometimes, a combination of stones work best, so you can always grow your stone selection as you add new tools to your workshop.

Chapter 7:
Finish it the Right Way

Finishing your masterpiece with an oil or lacquer protects the wood from dust, grime, and decay. Additionally, it intensifies the wood grain by enhancing the different hues and textures. Two types of finishes are popular among woodcarvers: surface and penetrating finishes. While surface finishes are easy to apply, it remains on the surface of the wood only. However, a penetrating finish is more durable, as it infiltrates the wood grain.

Secret Thirteen: Finishes add aesthetic quality and protect your pieces. Don't be afraid to play with several colors and textures, but, be careful of how you mix them. Putting one type of finish over another can destroy your hard work completely.

Surface Finishes

Applying a surface finish protects the exterior of a piece and does not penetrate the wood. These finishes include varnish, shellac, and lacquer. Most have a natural appearance, although some finishes may darken the piece. Surface finishes are easy to apply, which makes them a popular choice.

Varnish

Varnish is oil-based with additives including solvent and resin, which provides a transparent finish to the wood. The gloss option provides a shiny surface finish, while the satin and flat options dry to flatter colors through the addition of flattening agents. Always mix flat and satin varnish before application, as the agents settle to the base of the tin. Apply varnish over bare, stained, or painted wood. Although it can be used before a wax coating, the varnish will not adhere when applied over surface wax or in conjunction with other varnish brands (Ellenwood, 2008, p. 420). Although varnish dries slowly, it provides protection from UV light making it an ideal choice for many products.

Read the label on your chosen product for specific application instructions. Always clean your workspace before application otherwise dust is trapped within the varnish and creates a rough finish. A natural paintbrush, rag, or roller is suitable for varnish application. A warmer day is best for applying varnish, as cold and humid conditions slow the drying time. A very hot day is not ideal either since bubbles form on the surface when the varnish dries too quickly.

Apply a thin coat of varnish and leave it in a clean area for a 24-hour drying period. Apply a thicker second coat and additional coats, letting the piece dry fully between applications until you are satisfied with the finish. Most pieces require two to three coats, as varnish is a thicker finish. If your first coat has imperfections or rough patches, then use a very fine grit sandpaper.

Water-Based Varnish

Water-based varnish is a great choice if time is running out on your project, as it dries quickly and has very little odor. It is suitable for use over any dry surface or underneath wax. However, it does not do well on wet surfaces or when combined with other varnishes (Ellenwood, 2008, p. 422). Water-based finishes are thin and dry to a clear film with a natural feel, which lends it to many purposes. Most water-based varnishes do well on indoor items but it is not always suitable for items being used outdoors, as it is not heat-resistant.

Apply a water-based varnish with a rag or brush (preferably with natural bristles). Always stir your can of varnish, as shaking it creates bubbles that ruin the final product. Alternatively, purchase a spray varnish for faster application but shake it properly to mix the contents. Spray varnish creates a very thin layer over the wood, so it may require several coats for a proper finish. The thin consistency of water-based varnish may cause it to run down the wood if you apply a thick coat. Rather, take your time in applying four to five thin coats, leaving ample time for each coat to dry before the next application.

Shellac

Shellac is a wax-based finish sourced from bugs that live in trees. A variety of colors sets this surface varnish apart from others and dries to a glossy finish. Apply shellac over bare wood, varnish, alcohol-free stains, and paint. Shellac does not agree with alcohol, so never apply an alcohol-based finish over it. Additionally, do not apply shellac when the weather is humid or on damp wood (Ellenwood, 2008, p. 425). Shellac is quick-drying with an easy application process.

Shellac has sealing properties, making it an ideal choice for many projects. Scraped from trees, this bug secretion is flaky after processing but mixing it with alcohol creates the wax. Most shellac comes premixed, so you do not have to mix it all. However, you can purchase the flakes alone and make your wax mixture.

Apply shellac with a brush or pad it on with a thick rag. Shellac dries rapidly, so apply it liberally to prevent any missed spots. Some woodworkers apply shellac with a brush then run a rag over it immediately after application to remove any imperfections. Sand the piece with a fine-grit paper and remove any dust with a clean cloth before applying a second coat. Apply up to five coats for a glossy finish or sand it with super-fine paper to create a satin finish. Shellac may dry to a white film but this is rubbed off with a soft, clean cloth.

Lacquer

Lacquer is a solvent-based option and very thin, which enables rapid drying. After application by spraying, it penetrates the wood more than other surface finishes and enhances the wood's natural grain. Apply lacquer over bare wood, water-based stains, or shellac. Seal the wood with lacquer before applying stain or wax, but never use it with oil-based stains or varnish (Ellenwood, 2008, p. 428). Most lacquers contain tree resin, although modern variants combine it with nitrocellulose, which is another type of resin.

Lacquer application is done by either a brush or spray. If you decide to use a brush, then purchase a natural-bristle brush and apply a thin coat. Do not brush over the same area repeatedly, as the lacquer becomes sticky. Rather, work quickly, let the lacquer dry, and then add additional coats. Lacquer sprays come in aerosol bottles or as a liquid for spray guns. Whichever one you choose, apply a thin, even coat and allow to dry before adding more coats. Spray-based lacquers contain solvents with strong odors, so only apply them in well-ventilated areas and away from fire.

Paste Wax

Paste wax is an older option but remains popular among woodcarvers. Although it requires extra elbow grease, the application is easy and the costs are low. Paste wax works over any finish or bare wood, but do not use it as a bottom coat under varnish. Although the wax is solid initially, dissolve it in a mineral-spirit solvent or toluene to make a paste for application (Ellenwood, 2008, p. 430). Paste wax is made from beeswax, paraffin, Carnauba wax, or other agents.

Wax comes in many colors, so you have a range of options to finish your piece. Select a wax that has a similar color to your wood. This matching produces the best possible result, as using darker or lighter wax may not look as great. Use a clean cloth to apply the wax in a motion similar to polishing your shoes. Wax does not dry completely, so leave a minimum of 24 hours between applications. Most pieces only need one or two coats. Sanding between coats is not recommended because the wax remains damp.

Stain

Wood stain is another surface finish but penetrates the wood and changes the color. The purpose of stain is to darken the wood's color so that it makes the grain more visible. However, it does not protect the wood and requires additional surface finishing for wood nourishment and protection. Apply stain to bare or sanded wood but do not use it as a top coat, as it provides no protection for the wood.

A stain is a great option when your current piece does not match other furniture and trims in your home. When applied over lighter woods, stains provide a rich tone and change the color; that is why many stain colors receive their names from other trees. Apply wood stain with a brush or clean muslin cloth. Work quickly to avoid dripping and leave the stain to absorb into the wood for several hours. Afterward, wipe down the entire piece using a clean cloth to remove any unabsorbed stain, then let the piece dry.

Penetrating Finishes

Penetrating oils are a favored option by woodcarvers as it has many advantages. Besides giving a natural finish, penetrating oils enhance the grain, do not cause build-up, and provide a low luster shine, which looks similar to satin. A major benefit of penetrating oils is that the finish does not peel or crack, making it a kitchen and child-friendly choice.

All wood contains natural oils but these oils dry out over time. Finishing your wood with a natural oil replaces the wood's original oil and provides nourishment. Once applied, the oil penetrates the wood grain and settles into the capillaries. Afterward, the oil hardens (called self-polymerization) through an oxidation process. Yet, it does not become as hard as surface finishes.

Wood pieces that are handled infrequently work well with penetrating oils. Think about picture frames, wood trims, sculptures, and display cabinets. These items are not used daily, so a penetrating oil is great to keep them in pristine condition. However, most penetrating oils are free from or low in volatile organic compounds (VOC), so they are used for kitchen utensils, cutting boards, and wooden toys that sometimes travel to a child's mouth.

Penetrating oils come in three types: pure, polymerized, and hardwax.

- Pure oils are 100% natural, food-safe, and dry slowly. Apply the oil to bare wood and leave it for about 15 minutes, then wipe off any residue. Repeat this process five to eight times. It can take several weeks for the piece to dry properly, so do not rush the process.

- Polymerized oils dry faster, are food-safe, and shinier. Manufacturers complete the polymerization process by heating the oil without any oxygen. Apply polymerized (sometimes called boiled) oil onto bare wood and wait at least 15 minutes, then remove any residue from the piece. You can apply additional coats but it is not necessary. Give your work a couple of days for drying.

- Hardwax oils are a blend of vegetable oils and other components, such as beeswax. It creates a wax-like finish, has water-resistance, and dries quite quickly. However, a damp piece is not food-safe. Only use the finished piece for food preparation purposes once it dries completely.

Linseed Oil

Linseed oil is the first choice of many woodcarvers. It gives a classic, plain appearance to the wood while maintaining the original color. It prevents unnecessary cracks by strengthening the interior and exterior of the piece.

There are pure and boiled linseed options. The boiled variety dries much faster, usually within 18 hours. It is water-repellant and stops chalking, which makes it a great choice for finishing antiques and furniture. The drying agents can be abrasive, so use gloves during application.

Danish Oil

Danish oil is a suitable option for products stored indoors. This oil permeates wood deeply and works well on tight grains. It might include a varnish agent to promote shine. Some Danish oils have a walnut color, which adds warmth to the wood but does change the color slightly. Successive applications are required but may darken the color more, so some use it for initial applications and then use other oils for later coats. Most Danish oils are polymerized varieties, so always check the labels if you seek pure oil.

Teak Oil

Teak oil is a possibility for challenging woods, such as teak, mahogany, and rosewood. Deep penetration of the oil nourishes the wood without leaving a film on the surface. It is a quick-drying oil with properties that make it UV and water-resistant. These qualities make teak oil ideal for use around water features and maritime purposes but do not submerge the wood. Some teak oils darken the wood slightly and are unsuitable for softer woods. Teak oil works best when applying it with a cloth, although some people use a brush.

Tung Oil

Tung oil is suitable for use on its own or as a complementary product for other finishes. It is a clear oil with less gloss than other varieties, which provides a classic finish. Wood or carving imperfections are hidden when applying teak oil, as the satin finish lessens their appearance. Teak oil resists mildew and water, which makes it a versatile product. These qualities of teak oil often make it a great choice for the reconditioning of finished items.

Mineral Oil

Mineral oil differs slightly from other oils. It does not oxidize and cannot dry, as it is a petroleum distillate. Mineral oil repels moisture, is non-toxic, and does not change the color of the wood. It is suitable for use on toys and kitchen utensils. However, mineral oil continuously requires reapplication as it washes and rubs off easily. Some people use mineral oil with wax to make it last longer.

Walnut Oil

Another carver's favorite is walnut oil. Most walnut oils are non-toxic and safe for use on food items, so use it on utensils or butcher blocks. Walnut oil does not darken the wood but rather restores natural grain. It lasts longer than mineral oil and dries faster, as additional ingredients speed up oxidation. The finished product has a satin-feel and works best in warmer conditions.

A word of caution. Generally, most finishes are food-safe but that does not mean all of them are suitable. Always read the label on your specific product to check what it can be used for. Quick-drying products usually contain agents that make them unsuitable for use in food preparation or children's toys. Double-check the instructions and cautions on your products, especially if you have not used them in some time.

All wood pieces require care to maintain it in pristine condition. Whether it is a butcher block, toys, a rocking chair, or kitchen utensils, they require some attention once in a while. Goods handled frequently need more conditioning, but you should be able to tell when it is necessary. Recondition any item that appears dry by applying a generous amount of oil. Choose the best option for your masterpiece and apply a suitable finishing product. Leave it to dry and then display it in all its glory!

Chapter 8:
Get to Work

It is time to put your new skills to the test! You have all the knowledge you need to attempt a myriad of projects. Try your hand at the following projects that use whittling basics and the wood carving techniques shown in the first two chapters. Be patient while carving because you are still learning the skills. Do not take the process too seriously; rather, focus on making the cuts correctly and practice with several tools.

Secret Fourteen: Plan ahead before you start carving. Sketch out your design and do some research. Always use a cheaper piece of wood to practice cuts that you will make later on in the project rather than ruining your masterpiece.

Happy Mouse

Figurines, comic book characters, and animal silhouettes are great templates for incised carving. For this design, a happy mouse is at the center of the creation but instead of just a silhouette, additional details like a face and clothing are added. Practice the design on a cheap piece of softwood before carving it into a hardier wood, or keep it on softwood like balsa for painting later on. Start with a smooth piece of wood measuring 4" x 4" x ⅓".

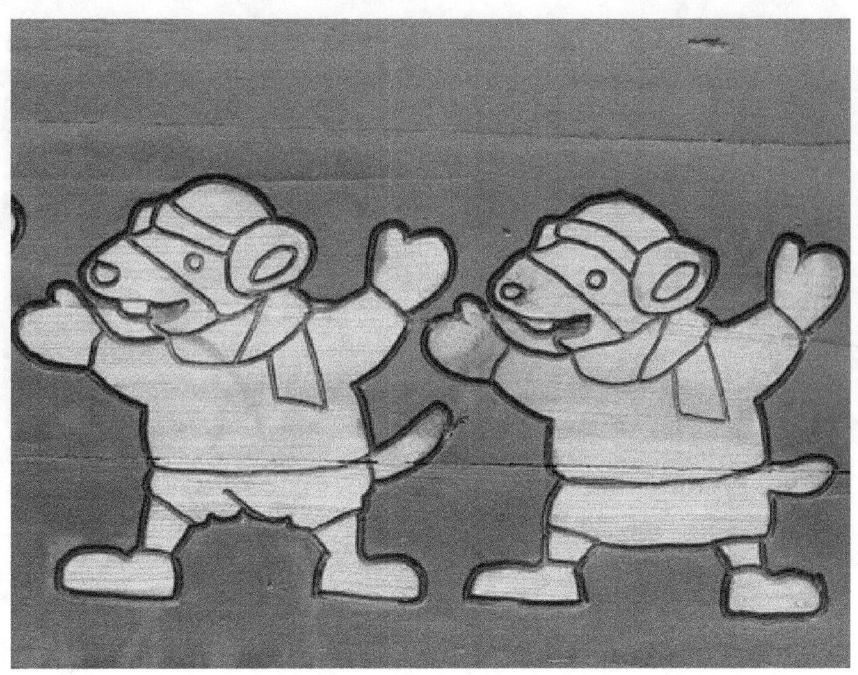

Instructions

1. Find a picture of a mouse, or use the one shown, as a template and transfer it to the wood.

2. Use a detail knife to make an initial cut around the exterior outline then carve the outline deeper with a veiner.

3. Carve the interior details like the scarf, shirt, and boots with a detail knife then use precision cuts to carve the facial features.

4. Go over any lines that you want to define more and check that the outline is slightly thicker than the interior detail lines.

5. Finish the mouse in any way you want. The one shown
   has a painted background, dark stain in the incised
   lines, and a natural finish to the main image.

Coaster Set

Drink coasters are ideal for practicing your new wood
carving techniques, especially incise carving. You can use any
type of wood and harder options work too because of the
greater control in carving finer details. Additionally, coasters
require less wood for carving providing a cost-effective first
introduction to intermediate wood types like mahogany. The
instructions for this set of coasters use square blanks, but
you can also make round or polygon-shaped blanks. The
sky's the limit with coasters so dream big! Most coaster sets
contain four or six in a pack but you can carve more or less.
The design for this set is not set in stone; you can use any
line pattern you want! Start by getting together six pieces of
wood measuring 3 ½" x 3 ½" x ¼".

Secret Fifteen: *Don't be afraid to sketch your own
designs. While there is nothing wrong with copying
patterns and projects, drawing your own ideas can make
you a better carver. You will start thinking more about
proportions and dimensions, and boost your creativity.*

Instructions

1. Use a pencil to draw a ¼" border on the inside of each
   blank. Make a second border by drawing the lines a
   ⅛" from the inside of the first border. Draw a third
   border a ⅛" from the previous one. You should have
   three borders in total.

2. Draw any design in the middle of each coaster. You can use the same design on all six or use a theme to create a different design on each coaster. For example, you may want a geometric theme, so draw a five-pointed star on one coaster, a double-pointed arrow on the next coaster, and so forth. Another theme could be fish and might include sharks, pufferfish, and bass.

3. Use a thin veiner to score the second border. Use long strokes and a low grip to carve a straight line. Next, use a detail knife and cut into the first and third borders. These borders should be thinner than the one in the middle, which creates a contrasting pattern.

4. Cut out the central design on each coaster using a detail knife or veiner. The choice is up to you, so decide whether you want a thin or thick incise carving. Play with several options until you find something you like. Just remember that you can widen the cut from a detail knife by running it over again or using a veiner but you cannot add wood once you make a wider cut.

5. Check that your incised carving has equal depths across all cuts by using a gauge such as a toothpick or a thin metal plate.

6. At this stage, the incised carving of the design is finished. You can add extra details to your design as you see fit. One idea is to change the square corners into round ones by using a microplane or rasp to remove the angled corner.

7. Sand the coasters and remove any stray wood slivers. Add a finish of your choice: paint the incised cuts, add

a contrasting stain, or leave it as is. Finish the coasters with a protective, water-resistant coating as you will be placing glasses with liquid on it. You may want to apply a maintenance finishing coat every few months for durability.

Bottle Holder

Most people have at least one bottle of wine in the house and this bottle holder is ideal for holding your wine. Alternatively, use it to hold your bottle of olive oil or balsamic vinegar. This bottle holder has an intricate chip carving design, which looks difficult but is quite easy to carve thanks to the repetitive pattern. Use a piece of butternut or balsa measuring 12" x 3 ½" x 1", as it is easier to carve. Below is the pattern for the holder. You will need a detail knife and chip cutting knife with a thin point for this project.

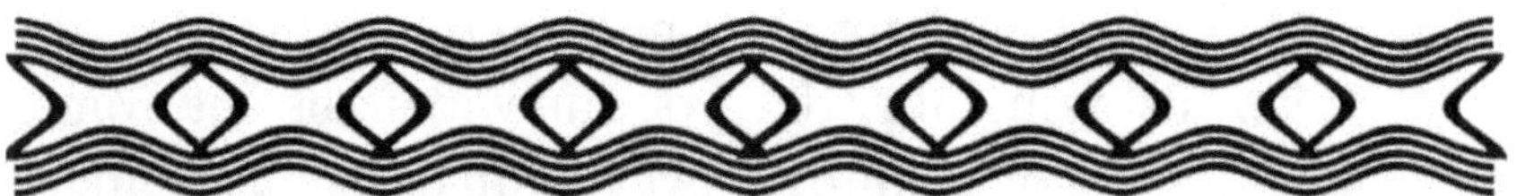

Instructions

1. Cut an angle into one of the small sides to form the base of the holder. The base should be cut at an angle of 37 degrees.

2. Cut a circle at the top of the holder (opposite the cut base) for the bottle's neck to fit into. The hold should have a diameter of 1 ⅜" and be located about 1" from the smaller top side. You can either carve the hole by hand using gouges or do it faster by drilling a hole with a power tool.

3. Draw a rectangular border that is ⅛" wide on all the sides of the block. Use a detail knife to create a very shallow scoring cut all around. Also make a ⅛" border around the circle on both sides.

4. Transfer the pattern to the lengthwise edge of the larger flat face that will be the front. Transfer it all along the block by moving the pattern to fit snuggly below the previous one; you want the curves to lie inside each other. Hold the wood with a quick-change clip as you transfer the pattern to the wood. It frees up both hands for working and secures the pattern to ensure it does not move and skew the design.

5. This pattern will be chip-carved using a series of cuts, as explained in the relevant chapter. Make a stop cut along each long wave using a detail knife. Try to do it on the right of each line, then use a chip knife to do free-form chip cutting along the wavy lines. Take your time in making each cut, as the angles change. However, the softer wood and a thin cut make it possible to remove the chip in a single glide. Repeat this process with every wavy line.

6. Next, we will start the second series of cuts, which will remove the diamond shapes between the waves but first, you have to create stop cuts. Make a straight wall cut along one side of each diamond. Remember that series cutting requires you to cut the same side of each diamond in the pattern before starting on the next side. Once you are done with one side of the diamond, move to the third and fourth sides. These straight-wall cuts will be used later in the design.

7. Move onto the actual diamond removal by using the four-sided hand position. Keep a very small area (ridge) between the previously made straight cut and the diamond chip. Once again, work through the diamond in a series method, rather than removing the entire chip in one go.

8. Now remove the hour-glass shaped wood between the diamonds and the waves by using the sloped plane to straight-wall method. Keep using the series method for consistency. The entire front should be carved at this point in time.

9. Repeat steps four to nine on the back panel of the bottle holder. If you are up for a challenge, you can chip carve the pattern into the sides as well for extra detail. In this case, you will place the pattern in the middle of the facing side rather than repeating it several times.

10. Tap the wood lightly against your hand to remove any stray chips. Use rifflers and needle files to smooth out the cuts then go over them with fine sandpaper. Apply a satin-finish lacquer for protection. You can use a paintbrush to apply a darker stain into the wave areas for extra accentuation.

Decorative Box

Chip carving is a staple technique on all types of boxes such as jewelry boxes or storage containers. Many elaborate designs can be carved into boxes. Some designs have only a few details, while others consist of many triangles, circles, and other shapes creating a complex design. For this project, you need a wooden box to carve into and the panels should be at least a ¼" thick. You can build your own box too but a pre-assembled box is suitable. Choose a box made from softwood so that you can carve the design easily. A bar or pipe clamp can be useful for holding the box while you are busy carving. However, rubber bands or web clamps work well to secure the box to a workbench.

Instructions

1. Find a piece of paper that is the same size as the top of the box to draw a design on. This design will be transferred to the top of the box once you are ready to start carving. It is not advisable to draw intricate patterns directly onto the wood, as it is difficult to correct lines drawn in mistake.

2. Design a pattern for the top of the box. It can be anything you want but try to include both a fine triangle and free-form carving elements. For example, you could draw a circular, mandala type design in the middle of the lower half of the box with curves and spirals around it. Alternatively, draw a decorative series pattern across the diagonal and add leaves around the sides of the diagonal stripe. Transfer the pattern to the top of the box.

3. Start carving the design by making straight wall cuts where necessary and score any lines where chips will be removed.

4. Use a chip knife and the three or four-sided method to remove geometric objects. Always work in a series form by cutting into one side of the shape throughout the entire pattern and then moving onto the next side.

5. Next, make free-form cuts for any swirls and curved
    elements in your design. Try to tap a chisel or gouge
    with a mallet for extra cutting practice with different
    tools. Keep your angles at relevant levels and do not
    apply to much force.

6. Check the depth of your cuts with a gauge and correct
    those that are not deep enough. Keep in mind that
    chip carving preferably requires a single cut into each
    line, as subsequent cuts may remove too much wood
    and spoil your design.

7. The carving on the top of the box is complete. You can
    leave it as is, or add decorative elements to the sides
    of the box, according to your preferences.

8. Use needle files and rifflers to clean up the inside of
    each cut pattern and line. Aim to get into all the tight
    corners for a perfect finish.

9. Finish the box by adding a stain with a coat of wax or
    oil.

Wall Sign

Sign making uses many carving techniques. The
alphabet project in Chapter 2 used relief carving but some
signs have the text going into the wood, which requires
intaglio techniques. Remember that chip carving forms part
of intaglio, so most intaglio projects have elements of chip
carving at some stage. Choose any word of your liking for
this project. I have chosen the word "Friends" for my sign,
although "welcome" and "love" are popular options too. This
is the ideal opportunity to use a harder wood, such as cherry
or mahogany, and you need a piece cut to 12" x 4" x ½". If

this design seems too small, then use a larger font and tools that suit you better.

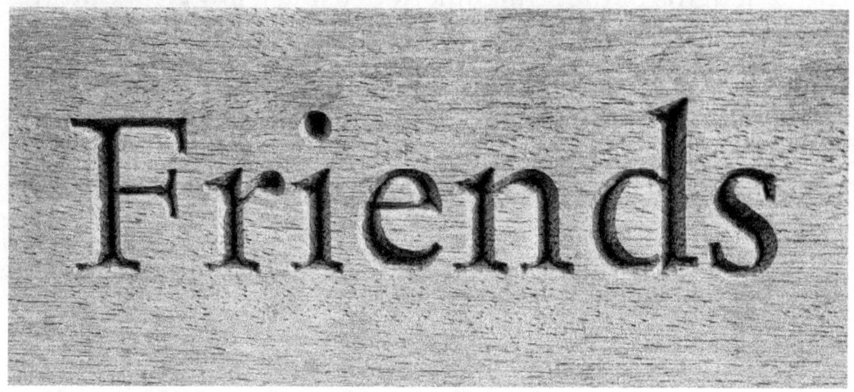

Instructions

1. Select your wood and change it to a font with some more details. A serif font that has little corners is a great choice to practice fine carving details. Print the pattern and transfer it to the wood.

2. Draw a ½" border and a second border ⅛" from the first on the front of the panel to create a frame for your design. Use a v-gouge to cut a square trough by making long shallow strokes. First, place the tool at an almost perpendicular angle to the left side and make a cut. Second, change the angle so that the blade is at an almost perpendicular angle to the right side. Finally, finish the square trough by cutting down the middle of the trough to define the angle of the cut border.

3. You need both hands to carve this piece, so secure your blank wood to the workbench using a clamping device of your choice. C-clamps are a great option but you can use other clamps too.

4. Use a ¼" inch v-gouge with a 60-degree angle to carve the letters. Make single pass troughs along the lengths of the straight letters using a low grip. Cutting curves like in the "e" are slightly more challenging, so you might want to swap out the v-gouge for a rounded gouge that fits onto your letter and carve it at the relevant angles using the free-form chip carving technique. After making the first trough, insert a toothpick and mark it for a depth gauge to use in subsequent cuts.

5. Add the serif details to each letter by placing a thin gouge at an angle to the wood and tap it lightly with a small mallet towards the inside of the letter. Cut the dot for the "i" using the globe cut method.

6. Remove any wood slivers with rasps while focusing on getting into all the tight corners. For an extra feature, incise or chip carve a patterned border. Sand the rest of the wood and apply any finish you want.

Flower Panel

If you want to practice intaglio carving, then this project is ideal for you. It is a wood panel artwork that contains a variety of flowers to practice carving at different depths using a range of fundamental cuts. Select a softwood for this design or opt for tupelo or another light-colored wood as this piece is one that does well with paint. You do not have to use expensive wood, since most of the flowers no longer have the natural wood showing after painting. This wood panel is suitable for hanging as artwork, so choose a reasonably sized piece of wood, measuring about 15" x 10" x ¾". This panel is a larger size than you may be used to working with and the intaglio carving technique could push the panel along the workbench. Hold the panel to your workbench with suitable size clamps.

Instructions

1. Print flower templates from the internet that have a clear outline and some internal features. Choose five flowers to use, such as a daisy, jasmine flower, hibiscus, cosmos, and plumeria. You want to create a pattern that has flowers facing towards you, with separate petals and not too much detail. Transfer the flower patterns to the top half of the panel and alternate their heights for a bit of playfulness. Draw a stem and leaves onto the bottom half and add a few clumps of grass at the very bottom of the panel.

2. Remember the basics of intaglio is to carve into the wood and the items closest to your view in real life will be the deepest cuts. Start by carving the grass. Score each blade of grass on the outside and add a thin line to the middle. Next, make a very shallow cup cut from the middle to the one side of each blade of grass and a deeper cup cut towards the other side. The sides of the grass should be deeper than the middle as they are closer in an actual view. You can use different cutting depths for the grass as some blades are closer to the viewer than others.

3. Carve the first flower, which is a daisy according to this pattern, although you can use any flower since the steps remain similar. The anther is closest to the viewer and will be the deepest, while the petals have shallower cuts. Score a globe around the anther (inside circle) of the flower to create a stop cut, then use a medium gouge to make a globe cut. Next, work

on alternating petals and carve them using a single pass ellipse cut. Carve the remaining alternating petals in the same way but make your pass shallower than the previous one to create the illusion of depth. Carve the stem of the daisy by making a single pass through from between the grass and into the petals. The stem should be shallow. Carve any leaves using the same process as the grass blades, by making cup cuts. Use a veiner to add detail to the anther by making tiny dimples into the globe.

4. The next flower is a jasmine flower, which has distinct petals with a clear separation between them. Use a jasmine pattern that has five wider petals. Mark the anther first by making a small scoring circle and remove only a small bit of wood from it as the anther is the part that is the furthest away from the viewer. Next, carve each petal separately but note the changes in depth. The tips of the petals are closest to the viewer so they will be the deepest carved area. Initially, carve each petal by using the multiple pass ellipse technique, then use your detail knife to carve the tips of the petals deeper and taper them towards the anther. Carve the leaves and stem in the same way as you did with the daisy.

5. An open, front-facing hibiscus flower will have the pistil closest to you while the petals open towards the back and are the farthest away. However, the petals have a rounded shape with the inside of the petal being just as far back as the tips of the petal. Carve the petals first by making multiple pass ellipses for each petal. The petal must have a concave shape and be deeper along the middle. Work with one petal at a

time and look carefully at your template to see the overlapping petal. The overlapping side should be carved at a shallower angle than the other petal. Next, create the pistil by using a veining tool to cut a single pass through from the middle of the flower and curve it towards one side. Run the veiner over the line again from the middle to the tip to add depth, and then make another pass right at the tip to create the deepest area. Use the veining tool to add the stamen segments to the pistil. The stamen should be just as deep, or deeper, than the pistil. Carve the leaves and stem into the design.

6. Carve the cosmos flower by using a combination of the previous techniques. Make the anther using the globe cut shown for the daisy, then carve the petals using the instructions for jasmine. Pay attention to depth in the flower so that small details become present. Use a detail knife to add texture to each petal by cutting very shallow ridges from the anther to the tip of the petal.

7. The final flower is the plumeria, which has overlapping petals similar to the hibiscus. However, the plumeria's petals are narrower than the hibiscus and there is no clear anther. Score the petal lines where they meet on the inside of the flower as a guide, then carve each petal using the multiple pass ellipse method. Focus on depth and the overlapping petals to create dimension.

8. Once you are happy with your intaglio flower carving, use rifflers to remove any stray wood and to smooth out your design. Paint each flower in its traditional colors using acrylic paint and allow the paint to dry completely. Apply a spray lacquer over the entire

panel and leave it to dry for several days. The panel is ready to be mounted on your wall or presented to someone as a handmade gift.

Scallop Shell Paperweight

Carving shells enables you to practice relief carving techniques and round moldings. There are many images of shells to work from or keep a shell on your workbench for inspiration. This pattern is taken from a design by Cindy Joslyn (2017). A softwood like butternut is a great option, although you may want to use cherry wood as it has the same color interplay as shells. Start with a block measuring 3" x 3" x 1 ½", as this is a deep relief piece. Wood in itself is not heavy enough to act as a paperweight, so a metal USS ⅞" flat washer adds the necessary weight and a felt covering avoids the bottom of the paperweight from scratching your desk surface.

Instructions

1. Use a compass to make a 3" circle inside both squares then use a gouge to remove excess wood around the circle so that you are left with a blank. A #3 gouge with a width of ⅞" works well to remove the excess wood stock without requiring a mallet. Alternatively, purchase a round blank measuring 3" in diameter to skip this step.

2. Measure ¾" from the bottom along the side of the blank and mark it all-around to indicate the relief line. Draw a scallop shell onto one face of the blank. Center it in the middle. You can use a template or do a freehand drawing.

3. Use a detail knife to make a stop cut around the shell's edge. Use the same gouge as previously to carve away the wood around the shell until it is level with the cutting line. You will have to deepen the stop cut as you carve away the excess wood. Use a flat gouge or chisel to create a level ledge around the shell.

4. Draw the shell's feature lines onto the wood and add an extension of these lines around the shell as reference points. These lines in the shell are called rays.

5. Create a stop cut with a detail knife between the teardrop shell and the triangular wings. Now, use the leveling technique to carve the wings until they are only an ⅛" high.

6. Round out the shell shape with a pocket knife until it is the desired shape on all sides.

7. Make a stop cut along each shell cap, which is the horizontal line over the shell using a detail knife, then make a gouge cut along these lines to emphasize the cut. The shell usually has three cap lines.

8. Define the smallest ray section by making v-cuts along each using a detail knife. Next, work on the other ray sections until all have a v-cut running through the ray. Detail the curvature between the rays by making gouge cuts.

9. Use a veiner to emphasize the wings by adding three lines into each.

10. Turn the paperweight around and trace the washer's external circle onto the wood. Make a ⅛ deep stop cut

all along the circle then use the gouge to remove the wood inside the circle. The stop cut is a guide for depth but placing the washer into the recess will indicate if it is deep enough. The washer should lie flush (flat) with the wood and not protrude from it.

11. Glue the washer into the base then glue the felt piece to the bottom of the paperweight. Allow the glue to dry properly.

12. Finish the shell by applying linseed or danish oil with a paintbrush and check that you get it into all the thin cuts. Wipe any excess oil off the wood after an hour and let it dry overnight. You may want to add a second oil coat and then allow the piece to dry out over several days.

Bird on a Branch

Many relief carvings feature landscapes or scenes from nature. This design is no different, as it takes its inspiration from nature, and specifically, our beloved trees that produce wood. This project is a high relief carving of a bird sitting on a branch. It contains a variety of textures and methods, such as rounding and leveling. A lighter wood works best for this project, as it is painted afterward but you can use any type of wood if you want to retain the natural color. You need a block of wood measuring 10" x 6" x 1 ½" and this project includes chisel work, so keep those ready. C-clamps can secure the wood to your workbench while carving.

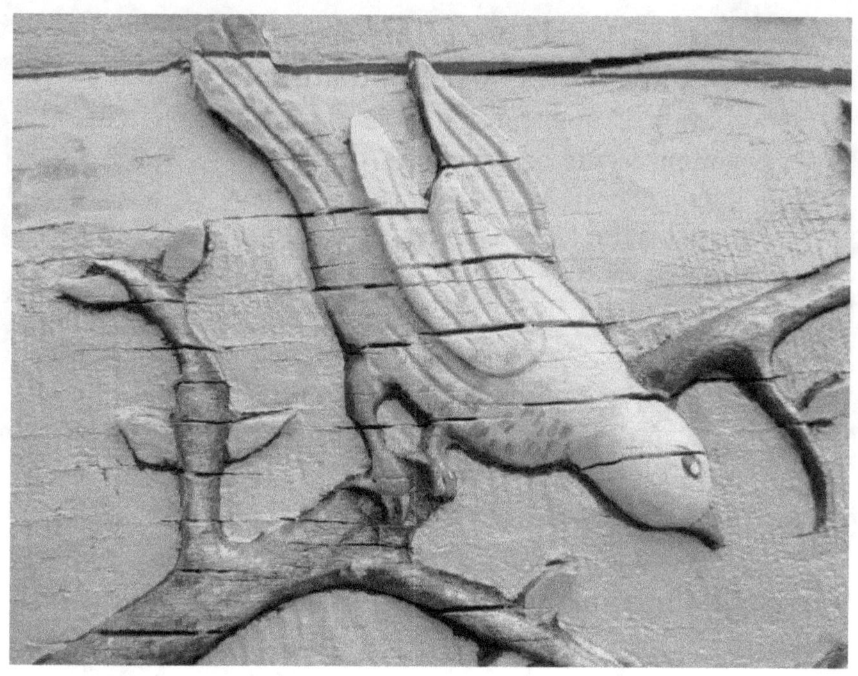

Instructions

1. Make a mark ⅔" from the top of each thinner side of
   the block and draw a line all around to designate the
   cutting level. Your relief carving will cut down this
   amount of wood from the top surface to reveal the
   design.

2. Transfer a pattern of a bird sitting on a branch to your
   wood. Extend the branches to reach the side of the
   block if necessary.

3. Make stop cuts all around the exterior outline of the
   design. The stop cuts can be relatively deep but do not
   force your chisel into the wood with excessive force. A
   light tap will suffice. Use a #3 ⅞" gouge to remove the
   wood around the design. Deepen the stop cuts when
   necessary and continue shaving off wood from the

background until it is at the ⅔" markings along the side of the board. Do not worry too much about creating a super flat plane, as ridging adds a textural element to the background.

4. Work on the leaves next to create the levels of the piece. Start by making a stop cut between the branch and each leaf. The leaves are thinner than the branch, so remove some of the surface on each leaf until it is ⅛" to ⅜" thick. The leaves can vary in height and have some slope to keep them looking real.

5. Use a detail knife to make stop cuts around the bird everywhere it touches the branch. Shape the branch by using gouge cuts to create roundness. The edges of the branch should be thinner than the middle section, so use a rounded tapering effect. Make any twigs or narrower branch sections thinner than the main branch but keep them thicker than the leaves. Add a slight v-cut into areas where the branches and twigs meet for added detail.

6. Mold the basic shape of the bird by making gouge cuts. Add stop cuts where the beak, feet, and wings meet the body, then continue carving the rounded body from this point. Keep the back wing thinner and remove extra wood from the head, neck, and tail to shape the bird properly. Once you are happy with the main body, shape the wings. Add v-cuts on each wing to denote separate feathers.

7. Use a detail knife to cut the beak and feet, paying special attention to the toes and beak line. Make a light dimple cut for the eye. Use a detail knife with a very thin point and undercut the feet, as well as the

twigs. These small details provide an extra dimension to the scene and set it apart from a simple carving.

8. Once all the shaping is done, use needle files to smooth out the carving and rifflers to get into the tight corners like the branch connections. Sand the background to smooth it out to your liking.

9. Paint the entire scene in colors of your choice. Although the scene above is fully painted, I sometimes leave the branch and twigs the original wood color for a special touch. Once the paint dries, add a sealing layer and let it dry out over several days.

Portrait with a Border

Why not try your hand at a project that uses several of your new techniques together? The Portrait with a Border project is a facial portrait made using relief, incised, and chip carving, which is surrounded by a gouged border. Natural colors work best for this project, so use a wood that has some color variation. Cherry or mahogany is a popular option since they have rich hues in the wood. These wood choices are slightly harder and more challenging to work with but this project is perfect for honing your skills with new techniques on more expensive wood. As always, practice your cuts, or the entire project, on a cheaper piece of wood before starting the final project. The raw block should measure 12" x 9" x 1 ½". A thicker wood block is fine too but it cannot be thinner, as you will be cutting into the top ¾" of the block.

Instructions

1. On the flat, top carving surface draw a horizontal and vertical line through the middle of the block. You should now have four rectangles. Using these rectangles as a guide, draw a large ellipse onto the block. The ellipse should touch all four sides and be slightly further away from the corners.

2. Draw another ellipse towards the inside of the first, ensuring that a distance of 1" is kept between the two ellipses. These ellipses form the border of the portrait, which will look like a picture frame once done. Draw similar ellipses on the bottom surface of the block.

3. Use a 7/8" wide #3 gouge to remove the wood around the ellipse so that you are left with an elliptical blank. Try to make the cut sides as flat as possible for maximum effect. Secure the elliptical blank to your workbench by using clamps of your choice. This project is an odd size and you may need to place the clamp directly onto the design, so keep a block of softwood between the work surface and the clamp.

4. Find a side-view portrait on the internet to use as inspiration for this project. Think about how coins often feature a side profile of an influential person's face - that is what you are aiming for. This project delivers a result similar to a coin. Transfer the pattern to the ellipse ensuring that the bottom of the pattern touches onto the inner ellipse but do not draw onto the frame. An older portrait where the person wears a hat or bonnet is a great choice.

5. Make a straight wall cut along the inner elliptical border and around the face's outline. Next, remove the background between the facial outline and the frame for the relief pattern. The background should have a depth of ¾" so use a ruler or gauge to check for consistency at various places.

6. Make a v-cut trough along the inner ellipse to define the picture frame. Use a ¼" #5 u-gouge to cut from the outer ellipse to the inside one all around the frame to create a ridged pattern. Make the cut by using the double pass trough method but angle the blade as necessary along the roundings.

7. Shape the facial portrait next. First, make straight wall cuts using a detail knife everywhere you have a line, such as around the eyes, mouth, hairline, collar, etc. Second, work on defining the face by making gouge cuts to round the head, nose, mouth, and hair. Next, focus on the finer details and carve the eyes and mouth. Finally, use free-form chip carving to detail the hair. Continue carving until you are satisfied with the scene.

8. Use a second cut file to make a rounded edge along the outside of the frame. Use the cross filing method to smooth it out from the top and remove the harsh edge. Then round the frame along the inner ellipse using a second cut needle file. Smooth out any ridges and slivers in the portrait by using needle files and rifflers until the entire carving is void of roughness.

9. Use sandpaper of various grits to finish the outside of the block and parts of the frame and background.

10. Apply a thick layer of paste wax with a clean cloth over the entire piece. Focus on getting it into all the ridges and small areas. It may take some extra time and elbow grease but the finished product is well worth it.

Birdhouse

Every woodcarver wants to make a birdhouse at some time during their carving career. A birdhouse is a great project because you can practice a range of carving techniques. This specific design uses incised free-form chip carving and relief carving. Choose to build the birdhouse yourself or purchase a kit that contains all the pieces for easy assembly. Alternatively, purchase a pre-assembled birdhouse.

Requirements

The birdhouse requires four wall panels, a bottom, and a roof. Here are the relevant sizes for each:

- Roof: 7" x 6 7/8" x 3/4"

- Front panel: 7 7/8" x 5" x 3/4"

- Back panel: 8 7/8" x 5" x 3/4"

- Sides x2: 8 7/8" x 5 1/2" x 3/4"

- Bottom: 5" x 4" x 3/4"

The sides of the birdhouse must be cut at a 15-degree angle from the back to create a forward slant. The roof then rests on the slanted slope for water to run off it in case it gets wet.

Additional items are required to assemble the birdhouse, including dowels, supporting wood, and hinges. Since assembly is beyond the scope of this book, instructions are not given but can be found by doing a quick internet search. You will also need acrylic paint in a color of your choice and another finishing product such as lacquer or varnish.

Instructions

1. Prepare one side of the front, back, side, and bottom panels by applying a coat of acrylic paint. Let the paint dry thoroughly before moving to the next step. Do not add paint to the roof.

2. Start by drawing a design on the front panel. A nice design is a bird perched on a twig with a thicker branch in the background. Add some leaves to the twig for extra details. Use a veiner or #10 gouge to carve the outline of the bird, then add some feathers using the free-form cutting technique. You do not have to make very deep cuts for the design to show through the paint; just ensure you cut through the paint. Use a thin, medium depth gouge to carve the twig. Carve the thicker branch in the background by making incised cuts with a detail knife and add some extra short lines for bark texture.

3. Work on one side panel at a time. Draw a design that consists of a thick twig with thinner twigs extending from it. Add two or three leaves and some berries to the end of each twig. Use a 45-degree v-tool to carve the main twig from the bottom of the panel and curve it towards the top. You can apply lighter pressure to make the v-cut narrower towards the front, or use a thinner v-tool as you move along the cut. Use a veiner

to carve the thinner twigs and leaves. You can change to a #9 or #10 gouge for thicker leaves. Carve the berries by twirling the veiner around its axis. Repeat the process on the other panel but the designs do not have to be an exact match at all.

4. The bottom panel is not carved so move on to the roof for which you will relief carve shingles. Draw horizontal lines ¾" apart across the width of the roof. Next, draw vertical lines between the horizontal lines to create the shingles. Alternate the line spacing so that the shingles fit together like bricks rather than in straight lines. Using a v-gouge and the low grip carve stop lines through the horizontal grid, then turn the piece to carve each vertical line. Use a wide, flat gouge to accentuate each shingle by carving away excess wood so that individual shingles emerge. Define the horizontal lines with a detail knife in the middle of each. Use a triangular needle file to sand away any wood slivers.

5. Assemble the birdhouse walls and bottom. Check if your carving needs some additional twigs where the wood joins and add those with a veiner or gouge. Add the roof to the house then apply a finishing like lacquer or varnish. A spray-type is easier to apply to a birdhouse but check that the finish you are using is water-resistant and offers UV protection. Let the piece dry and hang it in a suitable area to house birds.

Conclusion

I hope you are as excited as I am about wood carving! It truly is an amazing hobby with so many options for great projects. Basic whittling is a technique where you lose all track of time, as you carve out a handheld design. Now that you have mastered whittling, you are more than ready to move onto the intermediate projects in this book.

The first two chapters introduced four new techniques suitable for intermediate whittlers. These carving techniques are based on whittling and use similar tools. Incised and chip carving are fundamental to many wood carving designs, while intaglio and relief carving brings elaborate designs to life. Interestingly, all four techniques are connected in some way or another. Incised carving is the first step in most carving projects, while chip carving is a subset of intaglio. Relief carving is the opposite of intaglio as the carving protrudes rather than lying into the wood.

The different hand positions and grips assist in manipulating tools used for carving. Although the intermediate techniques use whittling knives, there are additional tools necessary for carving properly. Increase your tool collection with gouges, knives, chisels, and mallets for specialized carving. Accessory tools like clamps and files make finishing easier and assist in holding the wood while you carve. You do not need every tool in every size but a wide variety is a great idea, so build your workshop as you have funds available.

Woodcarving can be hard on the hands and cause fatigue. Gripping the tools incorrectly and using new tools may hurt your hands, so strengthen them by doing stretches or squeezing a stress ball. Knives and other bladed tools, even files with dull edges, can cause cuts and grazes on your hands. Consider using whittling gloves or finger guards to protect your hands. After all, cutting yourself will leave you out of action and unable to continue carving until your hand has healed fully. A pair of safety glasses do not go amiss either, especially when chip carving, as wood shavings and chips fly everywhere and may hit you in the eye, which can cause permanent damage.

Several types of wood are available for carving with the most popular options remaining softwood. Balsa, butternut, and basswood are suitable for beginners, although you may want to challenge yourself by using a harder wood like cherry or tupelo. Wood can be expensive, especially if it is hard to come by or a high-demand variety. Always practice your cuts on cheaper wood and only use more expensive wood once you master the new techniques. Be aware of grain patterns when purchasing wood so that your piece does not contain pith or too many interlocked patterns. There is nothing worse than ruining an expensive wood with an improper cutting from insufficient practice.

Sharp tools are crucial for proper carving as dull knives can split the wood or slip and cause unintended damage. A dull tool requires more force to move through the wood, which also ruins the finished product. Sharpening stones assist in keeping blades in good condition. Oil, diamond, water, ceramic, and Arkansas stones are available for sharpening and each has unique characteristics. Most carvers will have a range of sharpening stones to shape, sharpen, and polish the blade. Select a set of stones that work best for your tools and store the stones properly for longer usage.

A masterpiece is only as good as its finish. Finishing the piece requires careful sanding and application of a finishing medium. These mediums create a surface finish or penetrate the wood. Penetrating finishes are a better option as they nourish the wood and enter into the grain, while surface finishes produce a film over the wood. However, both types of finishes are suitable and you will know the best one for your piece. Be mindful of which finishes work with each other and those that cannot be used together. Try a variety of finishes on different pieces to identify the ones you like best.

Several projects are found in the first two chapters, as well as chapter 8. These projects contain various designs that span across all the new techniques. Some of the projects combine the techniques for more complex projects. Now that you have the knowledge and tools, grab a piece of wood, and start practicing your wood carving skills. Do not worry about failing, rather, try and try again, until you master every cut. You can only learn if you make mistakes, so take every opportunity to improve your carving expertise.

Throughout this book, I shared 15 secrets to wood carving. Remember these secrets and apply their teachings to carve successfully. If you enjoyed reading this book and have greater knowledge after learning these secrets, then please leave a review on Amazon.

References

Arbor Day Foundation. (n.d.). Anatomy of a tree. https://www.arborday.org/trees/treeguide/anatomy.cfm

Arnold, E. (2014). How to varnish wood… so it looks really good. The Daily Bark. https://www.wood-finishes-direct.com/blog/how-to-varnish-wood-so-it-looks-really-good/

Art of Making. (n.d.). Tool: flat chisel. The Art of Making in Antiquity. http://www.artofmaking.ac.uk/explore/tools/4/Flat-Chisel

Baylor, C. (2019a). How to apply a lacquer finish. The Spruce Crafts. https://www.thesprucecrafts.com/how-to-apply-a-lacquer-finish-3536491

Baylor, C. (2019b). How to apply finishing wax to a wood finish. The Spruce Crafts. https://www.thesprucecrafts.com/applying-a-paste-wax-wood-finish-3536492

Baylor. C. (2019c). How to use a skew chisel woodturning tool. The Spruce Crafts. https://www.thesprucecrafts.com/how-to-use-a-skew-chisel-3536930

Baylor, C. (2020a). Applying polyurethane for a durable, beautiful finish. The Spruce Crafts. https://www.thesprucecrafts.com/applying-polyurethane-for-durable-beautiful-finish-3536497

Baylor, C. (2020b). How to apply a beautiful shellac finish on
woodwork. The Spruce Crafts.
https://www.thesprucecrafts.com/get-beautiful-
woodworking-finishes-with-shellac-3536494

Best Wood Carving Tools. (n.d.). Complete comprehensive
guide for relief carving.
https://www.bestwoodcarvingtools.com/the-
complete-comprehensive-guide-for-relief-carving/

Duguay, C. (n.d.). Penetrating oil finishes. Canadian
Woodworking.
https://www.canadianwoodworking.com/tipstechniq
ues/penetrating-oil-finishes

Duncan, B. (2017). Great gouges: the essential tool kit.
Woodcarving Illustrated.
http://woodcarvingillustrated.com/blog/2017/09/04
/great-gouges-essential-tool-kit/

Ellenwood, E. (2008). The Complete Book of Woodcarving.
East Petersburg, PA: Fox Chapel Publishing.

Ellenwood, E. (2017). Anatomy of wood. Woodcarving
Illustrated.
http://woodcarvingillustrated.com/blog/2017/09/18/
anatomy-of-wood/

George Hill Timber. (n.d.). Understanding wood grain.
https://georgehill-timber.co.uk/blog/understanding-
wood-grain/

Infinity Tools. (n.d.). Choosing the proper mallet.
https://www.infinitytools.com/blog/2016/05/09/cho
osing-the-proper-mallet/

Irish, L. S. (n.d.a). Incised carving. lsirish.
    https://lsirish.com/tutorials/woodcarving-
    tutorials/woodcarving-fundamentals-
    techniques/specialized-techniques/incised-carving/

Irish, L. S. (n.d.b). Intaglio carving. lsirish.
    https://lsirish.com/tutorials/woodcarving-
    tutorials/woodcarving-fundamentals-
    techniques/specialized-techniques/intaglio-carving/

Johnson, D. B. (2006a). Intaglio. Canadian Woodworking.
    https://www.canadianwoodworking.com/plans-
    projects/intaglio

Johnson, D. B. (2006b). The bluenose. Canadian
    Woodworking.
    https://www.canadianwoodworking.com/plans-
    projects/bluenose

Joslyn, C. (2017). Sea shell paperweight. Woodcarving
    Illustrated.
    http://woodcarvingillustrated.com/blog/2017/07/06
    /sea-shell-paperweight/

Leenhouts, M. (2018). Chip-carved wine bottle holder.
    Woodcarving Illustrated.
    http://woodcarvingillustrated.com/blog/2018/04/23
    /chip-carved-wine-bottle-holder/

Lie-Nielsen. (n.d.). Fishtail chisels. https://www.lie-
    nielsen.com/nodes/4173/fishtail-chisels

McKenzie, B. (2016). Stylish birdhouse. Woodcarving
    Illustrated.
    http://woodcarvingillustrated.com/blog/2016/03/01
    /stylish-birdhouse/

Minwax. (n.d.). Staining interior wood.
    https://www.minwax.com/how-to-finish-
    wood/staining-
    wood/#:~:text=Stain%20can%20be%20applied%20w
    ith,fill%20deep%20pores%20with%20stain.

Pye, C. (2017a). Line carving: three simple styles.
    Woodcarving Illustrated.
    http://woodcarvingillustrated.com/blog/2017/09/29
    /line-carving-three-simple-styles/

Pye, C. (2017b). Basic relief techniques. Woodcarving
    Illustrated.
    http://woodcarvingillustrated.com/blog/2017/11/27/
    basic-relief-techniques/

Schroeder, R. (2010). Files, rasps, and rifflers. Woodcarving
    Illustrated.
    http://woodcarvingillustrated.com/blog/2010/01/24
    /files-rasps-rifflers/

Schroeder, R. (2017a). All about chisels, gouges, and v-tools
    part 1. Woodcarving Illustrated.
    http://woodcarvingillustrated.com/blog/2017/04/18/
    all-about-chisels-gouges-and-v-tools-part-1/

Schroeder, R. (2017b). All about clamps & vises.
    Woodcarving Illustrated.
    http://woodcarvingillustrated.com/blog/2017/12/08/
    all-about-clamps-vises/

Sharpening Supplies. (n.d.). Arkansas Stone FAQ's.
    https://www.sharpeningsupplies.com/Arkansas-
    Stone-FAQs-W169.aspx

Sharpening Supplies. (n.d.). Selecting a sharpening stone.
https://www.sharpeningsupplies.com/Difference-in-Sharpening-Stone-Materials-W51C116.aspx

Sharpening Supplies. (n.d.). What is the difference between ceramic stones and ceramic water stones?
https://www.sharpeningsupplies.com/What-is-the-difference-between-ceramic-stones-and-ceramic-water-stones-W135.aspx

Stewart, W. (2020). Best oils for wood 2020 - Reviews and buyer's guide. Wood Improve.
https://woodimprove.com/best-oils-for-wood/

Woodcarver. (2018). Best hook knives for easy spoon carving. Best Wood Carving Tools.
https://www.bestwoodcarvingtools.com/best-hook-knives-for-easy-spoon-carving/

Woodcraft. (2016). Wood for carvers.
https://www.woodcraft.com/blog_entries/wood-for-carvers

Woodworking Toolkit. (2020). Chip carving: Ultimate guides for beginners - tools, tips, resources & more.
https://woodworkingtoolkit.com/chip-carving/

Workshop Companion. (n.d.). Wood Grain.
http://workshopcompanion.com/KnowHow/Design/Nature_of_Wood/1_Wood_Grain/1_Wood_Grain.htm

Images in order of appearance:

https://pixabay.com/photos/clog-isolated-special-craft-dutch-18399/

https://pixabay.com/photos/carving-wood-mantel-hands-96088/

https://pixabay.com/photos/tool-wood-work-edit-carve-craft-1364892/

https://burst.shopify.com/photos/wood-working-tools-laid-on-a-bench?q=wood+mallet

https://pixabay.com/photos/annual-rings-tree-tree-grates-wood-2924661/

https://pixabay.com/photos/brush-oil-wood-paint-creativeness-5095758/

https://pixabay.com/photos/wood-figure-mouse-holzfigur-9247/

https://pixabay.com/photos/friend-carving-wood-friendship-1753870/

https://pixabay.com/vectors/border-decoration-design-element-40894/

https://pixabay.com/photos/bird-wood-carving-color-988415/

www.ingramcontent.com/pod-product-compliance
Lightning Source LLC
Chambersburg PA
CBHW071606030726
47593CB00001BA/333